T0196004

HOPE *To* END

The Housing Court Journeys

Van Hugo

authorHOUSE®

AuthorHouse™
1663 Liberty Drive
Bloomington, IN 47403
www.authorhouse.com
Phone: 1 (800) 839-8640

Published by AuthorHouse 01/02/2020

ISBN: 978-1-7283-4159-0 (sc)
ISBN: 978-1-7283-4158-3 (e)

Table of Contents

Those of you who read the previous book "Living in a Co-Op and the Journeys to Court", is that I leave trails behind on the credit part. I did so in case if the housing situation gets worst for me, the landlord and management brought the others and I in court for no good reason at all. However, I was the only roommate among the other three roommates who went in court. Before I go forward with everything in a chronological order, I want to say one thing about what happened one weekend of April 2018. The roommates (about three of them) who lived across us had the ceiling of the apartment collapsed on them. That happened early in the morning, and wondered if there were injuries involved after the aftermath of the incident. These roommates' apartment was the same as ours. That also raised the suspicion that our apartment and the rest of the apartments in the building had been done under poor maintenance, particularly the ones that rented out to roommates. The landlord and management spent money on cheap labor and material and expected to maximize their profit to higher extent. They could care less about the lives and safety of the tenants in those apartments, as long as they get money on rent every month, along with wrongful charges on purpose.

I wanted to go to see the magnitude of the damage before I went out that morning. I did not do so due to safety reason. I did not want to expose myself to chemical dust that would affect my health without any protection mask. The country continues to have mess up health care system and I had to protect myself from getting sick. One of our roommates did go in the apartment as soon as the problem happened, and the Fire Department was in the building in case if the problem happened to be worst. I heard the roommate said that this is a lawsuit against the building. I could say is that having the lawsuit is one, but wonder how many housing cases held in the housing court when the tenants happened to be residents from other states is another. These tenants happened to live in New York due to economic reasons. Therefore, their cases could be very hard to deal with in the housing court. If there is no problem at all, it could still be very hard for them to have lawsuit against landlords because the landlords have been protected and wonder by whom, by the lawyers and/or the system. The landlord's problem and issue had been around at the beginning of building the country, even before building the country which I mean to say across the world. Therefore, landlord has become part of the system in the country. One should definitely go back in the past to see that the problems of landlords and housing issues continue to remain in modern society. Therefore, there is no way to abolish landlordism effectively. One would never get what he or she deserves out of any court cases against the landlords because of the manifestation of racial prejudice, discrimination, power, right, privilege, and injustice that is going in housing court. One would never get what he or she deserved in housing court cases due to class and race issues. Even though one would get something, he or she may not get what he or she deserves. The housing court may not be the only court. It seems to be that it may happen everywhere in all of the court systems. I heard some people said that they had lawyers to help them won their court cases for about more or less than tenth of thousands of dollars. That is nothing when actually the landlords would get their money back on rent, particularly on rent hikes to higher extent if they continue to live in their apartments. Who knew how they get that little money for their court cases when actually they might get much higher than that for their court cases. I also wonder what kind of deals that these tenants' lawyers made behind closed doors with the landlords' lawyers to get lousy money for their clients. I mentioned in my previous book about that lawyers can meet with other lawyers without their clients knowing about it. These lawyers may not tell their clients what they really talked about behind closed doors. One of the sources that I included on the previous book stated that lawyers could make matters worse for their clients if the lawyers do not handle the housing court cases properly and effectively.

I remember one day, early year of 2018, I watched television and I stopped to one of the local government channel, listened to the Mayor talked. The Mayor said that he is about to go to Landlords to give up their buildings for rewards. Otherwise, the government would bring them in court if the landlords refuse the rewards to get the buildings from them. There are two things I want to say about that. The **first** thing is that where the Mayor is about to get the money to reward those landlords. I wonder if it is going to be the tax payers' money that the Mayor would use to do that. These landlords happened to be filthy rich already and it is absurd to keep giving them money. It seemed to me that history had repeated itself after the American Civil War. Some slave owners got money on insurance because the Civil War hurts their business. I also wonder where the Government got the money to pay these slave owners after the Civil War. What about the slaves who got caught up in the middle of everything. What the slaves got out of the Civil War? The cause of the Civil War was that it was based more on economic interests and less to save the slaves from bondage. The slaves got nothing, not only reparation and reward, but only Post Traumatic Slave Syndrome (By Dr. Joy Begruy) and the continuation of prejudice, discrimination, and injustice (horror and terror). These problems continue to happen or manifest in modern life or society. One has to prove to me what the slaves got and real amount of what they got out of the Civil War. Some or few of us should know about "Hate Crimes in the Heartland". There were few blacks who did the best they can to create economic opportunity on their own, without any help from anyone, until they were terrorized by those who did not want them to get ahead, by using rape as an excuse to make that happened. The result of the crime had led hundreds of blacks killed and thousand faced homelessness. I wondered what the government did about the crimes against the blacks at that time. The movie, Marshall, by Chadwick Boseman, was a great example since the movie based on true story. Thurgood Marshall saw what the system had been doing to the blacks due to unfair laws to punish the blacks for crimes they did not even committed and saw there should be drastic changes over all in the system. I saw the titles of all of his books and they all have scary and interesting titles.

All of us should know by now that some laws that have been implemented by the Government are there to protect all of us or discriminated against all or some of us regardless of class, gender, and race. Therefore, the problems of unfair laws at that time continue to manifest themselves in the country and in the world. They continue to happen heavily in some countries across the world. The problem that one's terrorized and sabotaged another economy has been going on for probably thousands of years. Some of the sabotages occurred through sanction and embargo. Some people have been struggled for thousands of years looking for their own states. They would never get their own states and the bloodshed continues, yet profits have been made on the bloodshed. Therefore, some of us would never get reparation. My home country is a great example of that despite the fact that some outsiders (foreigners) across the world had been benefited from the country in the past and continues to benefit from the country on the mess that has been going on, still care less about the country on reparation. Otherwise, I may be mistaken by everything I say there. I remember I watched "Like it is "one Sunday morning and these two African Americans leaders came to talk about what appeared as reparation. They went to speak with those who came from ancestors that use to have slaves. The black leaders asked them to free us because it is still stating on papers or documents that the blacks are still on slavery. They use their ancestors as an excuse not to do anything. They say to the black leaders that it would be disrespectful of them to go against what their ancestors did, in other words. There were two blacks who spent about thirty years in jail over a crime they did not commit. They came out free due to another investigation to find out that they were innocent of the crime. One of them said that he is getting out of the state. The other one said that they found a place for him to work and wonder what kind of job they offer him. They can offer him job, not reparation or reward for putting behind bars as black person under prejudice, discrimination, and injustice. There are a lot of cases like that of blacks had been accused of crimes that they never committed and wonder if those accusations happened wrongfully on purpose. There was a movie I watched by Steven Seagal. His wife was murdered at the beginning of the movie and sent to jail for six years. He was released after another investigation opened due to new technology that had been used on the crime scene this time. It has been found that he was innocent of the crime. The court offered him less than five hundred dollars as a reward. He found that it was disrespectful and insult of the court to give him that kind of money and decided to reject it with a mean on his face. It may have happened many times in real life if the movie gives an example of it. I spoke with someone while I was in school. The person told me that her country is doing everything for the interest of the United-States. Her country got a deal that is not good and not bad either. The person comes from in one of the countries in the continent of Asia. Therefore, the United-States and other Western countries in the world should be happy that the rest of the world is doing everything for them, instead of otherwise. Some countries around the world held some of U.S. debts. Some countries around the world did the best they could to look attractive just to be exploited to some degree. Among those countries had their economy sabotage by some outsiders (foreigners) who were there to maximize their profits and left mess behind, which they never clean. Therefore, these countries did the best they could on their own to thrive and hope for the best in the future. I hope my home country follow those countries examples and do the best they can to get themselves out of the problem that the country had been since the country's independence in 1804, with unfair debts and forced to pay the debts under corruption, extortion, and robbery. One should know by now about part two of the documentary of "An inconvenient sequel" that came out about a year ago. There is a big blow in the face of the United-States that we cannot blamed other countries that destroy the environment when actually we continue to do so for hundreds of years due to industrial evolution (so do the western on the same issue). Therefore, that would be hypocrisy. The United-States and the western world, who knows how many other countries around the world started like that to bring their countries into development. Otherwise, their country would suffer in this world. They added that the United- States and the Western world never follow through of what needs to be done to help out. That is the kind of treatment that some or most countries around the world have to deal with in the global economy. It is absurd of the current president to impose sanction and high tariffs to a country and later on asked the country to investigate government officials of his country. That seemed to be the cause of the American and British war because of high tariffs to prevent mass dumping of goods in another country to higher extent for profit purposes. Otherwise, the tariffs issue had been used as an excused or diversion to make up for other personal issues such as the car emission issue may have been one of those personal issues.

There is one thing I want to say to end this part to move on the housing issues. One should look at the world economy in some politicians' political economic term. These politicians views of the world economy is that everybody wins, but not equally which they would not tell you the facts out of that, but one must figure out of his or her own. If one knows about slavery well, he or she should know about what is going on in the world economy. These politicians mean that if one person makes one trillion dollars and the other one makes one billion dollars is a win on both sides that happens unequally. Therefore, there is a huge gap between that amounts. The problem that causes is who do more, less, or nothing at all to get what amount. That problem happens on both national and international level. That problem would remain in the world and there is nothing that can stop it. That is also bringing the matter of competition which happens under inequality on both national and international level. The north and the south did benefit from slavery to some degree despite that the slaves had been accused indirectly of competing unfairly with free labor men who thought they were free. Therefore, it is those free labor men continue to manifest themselves in national and international level maintaining some accusations that they do not have proof of, and the truth will be hard for them to comprehend. Therefore, there never had been a real competition, but only cheating, disaster, and inequality that come along with the competition. Those of you should watch "Untold History of the United-States", by Oliver Stone (2012). I recently found out about that documentary while I almost finish with the book. There is another person which I was shocked about to hear that he committed suicide was Michael Craig Ruppert. He had discovered a lot of what had been going which may have cause the unfortunate events of what happened in his life. He also stated that the bills are due for those who went to other places to destroy those places. I wonder if he meant the Western world. However, it seems to be that is what going. The opposite of what must be done is happening. Those who caused the problems determine not to do anything. They just keep building weapons to bring fear on those whom they owed and claimed that they are protecting themselves from terrorist, barbaric, savages, hostile, insurgent, and/or communist. No wonder they cannot tell you the truth about 9/11, but fabricating stories. I discovered about him in 2007 by miracle. He represented on stage a lot of scary classified information about scary businesses and mentioned about god (gold, oil, and drug). There is one thing I have to say about what the person said to me later which made certain things clearer. The person told me two things. The person told me that it is wrong when someone (outsider or foreigner) comes to your place and put weapon in your hand to find someone else that you never know anything about just to create enemies for yourself.

The person also added that it is also wrong when someone bad (outsider or foreigner) come to your place and puts up with another bad person to your place to create problems, trouble, and issues in the place. It seems to be that the ways things are in the world now is having small beginning. It is the small beginning which turn things the way they are and spread everywhere like cancer, virus, or diseases to higher extent.

There is a Haitian lawyer who did the best he could to create about seven hours of history on disks almost a decade and half or more ago. He focused on the most major events that affected Haiti (1492-2006). The former elected democratic president twice and overthrow twice stated that a lot of people's blood had been spilled for the country in the documentary "Aristide and the Endless Revolution" that I discovered in 2006 by miracle on dvd. The former president was right because those major events were the most important ones and affected the country in deep profound ways. I found out that at the end of 1800 or beginning of the 1900 that some Western countries used Christopher Columbus as an advantage to claim Haiti as their even though Christopher Columbus was not their ancestor or countryman. There was a small book I read about Christopher Columbus that he showed the others about America and betrayed later on by them if I remembered that was what happened. They told Christopher Columbus that they did not need him anymore and they took over from there. I was shocked to hear about those events and felt illiterate and ignorant which did not done by my side but to those who kept those events to themselves and might blamed me for not knowing about them, when they did not want me to know about them to begin with. The president did what he could to help minimize the poverty rate in the country. There was an independent source that someone sent me to my email address few months after the earthquake that occurred. It is the source that I began to find the real reason why they overthrow the president because of his agenda that he set forward to use the remaining resources of the country to help the country. I kept digging heavily about the cause of the earthquake when I found from someone that it was caused by manmade. I discovered a map miraculously about routes in the Caribbean. There were few spots that had dots and circles which they had their meaning. All of these earthquakes and hurricanes that had been occurred in certain countries in the Caribbean concentrated where those dots and circles had been placed on the map. The earthquake that occurred in Haiti one day of the summer of 1995 was a strange earthquake. I was taken lesson to be prepared for school and felt some strange sound deep underground before the earthquake happened. It felt that some kind of force and energy had been shooting deep underground and the earthquake lasted about five seconds (3. magnitude). I felt what happened underground because I was seating on the concrete while I was facing the board. I found that concrete can be echoed. I remember one of the episodes of unsealed: conspiracy files, is about the cause of the manmade earthquake and hurricane.

"I remembered probably at the end of the year 2017, probably on the same channel that the Governor made a speech. One of the issues that mentioned on the Governor's speech was that he stated that the City does not have money. Anyone with a lawsuit would be held responsible and accountable to pay for the lawsuit. The City would be unable to pay for any lawsuits. I wonder if the same thing applies to the housing issue since there has been a war going on between the tenants toward landlords, including Co-Ops, City Agencies, and public housings. It seems to be the reason why the people who got sick from working at the ground zero would never get anymore grant for their conditions, may have been done so due to that speech as well. I read two of the free newspapers that came out early of June 2019 about the same issue in congress. Congress stated that they are not responsible for that, it is a state issue, problem, matter, and concern. The articles stated that most of the congress members did not attend to the meeting. One of the famous talk show hosts were there represented some of the people who were affected about the cancelation of the grant's renewal. As for the Mayor, the Mayor has to prove where he is going to get the money to reward these filthy rich landlords. It seems to be that the reward would come as government's subsidies or Federal grant. Who knew how many landlords continue receive government's subsidies for decades. One of the presidents said behind closed to soak the poor, subsidies the rich. The Mayor even said on the same speech that he is about to shut down all shelters in the city and everyone would stay where they are permanently. I wonder where people are going to stay when they continue to face eviction by the housing court without any protection from the government and the court which causes the problem to them. I wonder what is going to happen to those who never pay rents for twenty, thirty years in Co-Ops, particularly the one that I was evicted from illegally under identity

theft, falsify information and documents, and perjury on purpose. Some of these people happen to be the board and their families who never pay anything for years, but acting as landlords.

I went to see a friend of my mother one day of June 2019. I explained to her briefly about the previous and the current housing issues that I had to deal with. The television was on and the new was on. While she was on the phone talking to some body and the housing situation happened to appear on the news. They were talking about public housing only. I found that it will cost about thirty billion dollars to repair nearly two hundred thousand units. I could say given the grant to fix those units is not the problem. The system could not afford to find itself in the same problem and issue that some people may take the money, probably not doing anything at all with the money and become filthy rich with the grant. I heard that one of the presidents of the country gave more money to help the public, than any other presidents. The money ended up in the pockets of those who were supposed to use the grant accordingly, but ended up take the grant for themselves and become rich. My home country and others suffered the same problem on grant relief that they never receive. Despite what the Governor and the Mayor said, the problem on the housing seems to never solve. We will never get a universal healthcare. I do not think we will get a universal housing. The problem for both would continue to remain no matter how the government would do to establish any new orders and laws on them. These problems would never be solved when the love and strong attachment for power, money, wealth, privilege, and right are continue to affect both of them negatively. Otherwise, I may be mistaken about what I just said there. It seems to be that it will cost about one or two trillion dollars (the actual amount may vary here) to fix all of the units that has been affected everywhere. I wonder how much it will costs over all on lawsuits toward the landlords and everyone else in charge of buildings per tenant."

It is the Black race, or African Americans in the country and in the world who will continue to suffer even though some and few of us would do what is right and best in this life. Otherwise, I may be mistaken about everything I said. I always say to my few black brothers and sisters that they have to do more than everybody else, just to get a little of something. They also have to do so appropriately, properly, effectively, respectfully without having anger and hatred in their hearts and minds. They have to go under deep incarnation in order to become somebody else, somebody new. It is effectively painful for us to let go off the past that we suffered under bondages and hardship, since our suffering are absolutely done by man-made under horror and terror. Let us do the best we can to forgive and remember. However, it was not everyone who agreed with what happened to us. Who knew how many of them helped slaves to escape slavery during that time despite the laws might imposed on them not to harbor slaves, and costed their lives. There was episode 12 of season 4 of original MacGyver that give some examples. Episode 13 was about another issue which also interesting as well. I used to watch these episodes back home as a child. I did not understand what were really going on in them. I am about over twenty years late on watching MacGyver and I got the chance to watch all seasons of it. The movie, Green Book, by Mahershala Ali and Viggo Mortensen, is another example since it based on true story. Despite all of the racial issues and problems that happened in the country, these two strangers find ways to appreciate each other and became good friends until death do them apart. I include few of the personal issues I had to deal with in this book which going to be on part two to prove this is what we have to deal with in life. The Authority (name of that Authority has been omitted for the purpose of the book), knew about some of them. Above all, I could say that we are all inherited everything that is going on in the world regardless our class, race, and gender differences politically, socially, economically, and religiously. Therefore, the aspects of politics, social, economy, and religious are that they connect, intertwine, overlap, and separate from each other at the same time. We are all also inherited everything that happened in the past, present, and future out of them. We are also inherited the good, bad, and ugly that come out of them, particularly the bad and the ugly, that is what have been going from the beginning of time. Above all, some of us, regardless class, race, and gender differences are continued to care for the world, do the best we can, and hope for the best. Despite the outcome of what the housing issues and problems might be, the tenants would suffer from post-traumatic housing syndromes. The tenants would remain on their own to deal with the symptom. Blacks or African Americans would suffer the most than anyone else.

"There was an ugly scene that I witnessed probably on the middle of September 2018, before I was evicted again illegally. I took the bus at Rogers avenue on my way back to the apartment. There were few Junior high school students on the bust talking loud and behave certain ways that appeared wild. They were few boys and few girls. One of the ladies appeared to come from the Caribbean, stood up and gave it to these Junior high school students. She said that this was the reason why Cops are killing us because of our attitude. One of the girls was mad about that and said to the others that she wanted to beat the lady up. The rest were mad, but not as mad as the one who wanted to beat her. I wondered if the girl was playing or not. This problem kept going until I got off the bus. There were few Caucasians, Latinos, and Asians witnessed everything. The bus was crowded as well. The lady was right about what she said. However, some people can effectively use the attitude problem as excuse, pretext, and advantage to accuse some of us who do not show it, to get us in trouble. I face that twice. I faced that from my previous employer because one of them accused me that I gave attitude when the other two did not see any attitude came out of me, even though they fired wrongfully on purpose over lies. The reason why I was accused of giving fake attitude was that I did not give them way out of the problem they created. I was accused wrongful again on giving attitude after the law firm was served. I was accused of that by our own sister who happened to be a lawyer when she could not find her way around with me. Attitude problem is human being problem regardless where they coming from around the world. It is always African Americans who get in serious problem and trouble with it. Some people show attitude as worse as ours, even worse than ours, but they never got into real problem that could make them lost their life in front of the Police. We must do the best we can to get our emotion and anger in control and do not let any ridiculous stupid things got us angry and upset. I remembered one Saturday morning of winter 2016 I was in the central library doing a personal work and studies. I was almost all the way in the back of the languages and literature section. I heard a huge noise of somebody who was sounded really angry, near the check in and out sections. The library is hollow and echoes. I went to find who was really that angry, but assumed that it could have been one of my brothers. However, I was shocked when I found out that it was a white male, around his thirties, was angry, furious, and yelling at security and wonder why. He was very angry, furious, and yelling as if he wanted to hurt somebody really bad. I asked one

of the security officers who were there about what happened to the gentleman. He responded by saying that he lost his house and homeless, they tried to help to go to place for help and the condition that the gentleman was in about his hygiene. The gentleman left before Police arrived, or if Police was called for that situation. It was on the second year of the homelessness I have faced when the incident happened. The person was just faced homelessness. I wonder what happened to him, he may have get help fast and easy than I do."

I remember I watched the news early year of 2018 that a building, probably located in Brooklyn, received about six million dollars on Federal grand every year. The building continued to be into ruin. The apartments remained without maintenance. However, if these apartments would get maintenance in the future, they would do so on cheap labor and cheap materials. The rent would effectively goes up to higher rate (about $1500 per month or more for one bedroom). I wonder if the Federal grant has been given to the building as a form of borrowing, so that the Federal government makes the government to pay for it. The **second** thing is that what kind of landlords that the Mayor will go after. I wonder if the Mayor will go after the big landlords or small landlords. I do not think all landlords are created equal under the landlordship. There are landlords who continue to remain anonymous and they do not want to be identified by authorities. I also wonder if the Mayor would go after the landlords all at once, or one at the time. There are about sixty to seventy percent of buildings controls by landlords throughout New York City **(the actual percentage may vary)**. I wonder how many landlords stay anonymous while running the buildings and maximize profits. I wonder how many of those landlords running their buildings on phony organizations, particularly phony organizations within phony organizations. I wonder if these cases would solve before the Mayor's terms come to an end. I wonder if the Mayor's predecessor would continue where the Mayor left off (Democrat or Republican). Therefore, it will be very costly to go after these landlords and may add up to the national debts of the country.

I also wonder which court system will hold all of these court cases. I wonder if it is going to be the Supreme Court, Judicial Court, or Civil Court which included the one in downtown Brooklyn. If all, few, some of these cases hold in downtown Brooklyn, nothing would solve effectively because the lawyers and clients do not have respect for the court and the Judges. Therefore, the court allows them to get away with crime and punishment. The court also let them get way with prejudice, discrimination, slavery, injustice, harassment, racial prejudice, corruption, robbery, extortion, identity theft, perjuries, pretense, falsify information and document, wasted of times, wrongfully accused on purpose, wrongful labels on purpose, serving people on their absences on purpose, serving people on the wrong zip codes on purpose, blame the victims for the problems, etc. The court allows the lawyers and clients to use anything as excuse, advantage, and pretext not to show up in court. The book would details about all of them later on. As I mentioned on my previous book about three lawyers who told me about coming to the housing court in downtown Brooklyn. One of them told me that not to become a lawyer because it is a nasty business. The lawyer may be referred to the housing court lawyers only. The other one told me that the downtown court would never do anything about my case. The third one told me that this is a small court and the case must go to Supreme Court. The lawyer added that the court or the Judge's decision was wrong, which makes me wonder which one of the court decisions was wrong. There were two decisions. The lawyer told me that I did not do anything which the lawyer was wrong about that. The lawyer ended up robbed me of seventeen hundred dollars, gave me a worthless, shitty, and useless appeal. The lawyer told me that he could not represent me because the judge would say to him that he should not be in court, it will be a waste of his time. The lawyer added that if the worthless, shitty, and useless appeal worked, came back to him so that he would charge me more for the case. The lawyer ended up blame me as the victim when I asked him my money back. The lawyer accused me of trying to vacate the Judge's decision, and advised me not to do so, which was a lied. The lawyer never asked me to see my exhibit and response collected in court, but only read the Judge decision and gave me wrong definition of the court paper or decision. The lawyer never told me that the lawyer(s) and their clients went against the Judge's decision which turned out to be disrespectful for them. Therefore, the lawyer knew effectively that he could not do anything about my case and stole my money. I would not waste my time to go to another lawyer for the current case because I may find myself into the same problem. Therefore, one would always get evicted without any protection from the court, even though one would win the court case. The previous case and current case I had to deal with turned out to be that way. The lawyer charged $1700 dollars on part of the Judge's decision *(The court holds that the foregoing was insufficient to demonstrate a right to possession of the premises or a right to succeed to his father's tenancy).* I simply stated on the response collected in court before trial that I share responsibility with my father. The board even accused me saying that they evicted me because I tried to take the apartment for myself. One of the board's member relative told me about that when he saw one day of November 2014 walking in the area, on Flatbush Avenue. I just simply wanted the apartment to be on my father's name until the illegal eviction took place and messed up everything which the lawyers and the board were the ones who caused that to happen. I did the best I could to fix things when they were the ones who came around to destroy them.

"Speaking of wrongfully accused on purpose, it has been going on since the beginning of time. I have been wrongfully accused on purpose a lot in the previous court cases. I began to pay more attention to that on the current court case and decided to include it in the second book. Who knows how many people died and sent to jail over accusations that had been done that way? Who knows how many countries around world continue to be accused that way for political and economic purpose which led to war, invasion, and civil war? I began to see that wrongfully accuse on purpose is one of the worse type of accusation. I have been wrongfully accused not in the court cases, but also at work and among friends. I always do the best I can to protect myself from any type of accusations done that way. Therefore, wrongfully accused on purpose is the worst type of accuse that is done under prejudice, discrimination, injustice, and racial prejudice."

I mentioned in the previous book that I may be the only resident of New York City among the other three roommates. I also wonder if few, some, or most of the apartments people are paying a lot of money for the whole apartment or rooms had been built under cheap materials and cheap labor. After what happened to the roommates who live across us, I began to worry about my safety. I do not want to be victimized by the apartment and the lousy room I rented for a lot of money. I mentioned on my previous book that I used to hear noises of fallen material thought the ceiling of my room, right by the window. The sound that the fallen material was loud enough, as if someone hurled pile of dirt or tiny grains to a metal that could easily make huge sound. Rain got into my room when it pours out heavily due to leakage. Another problem that happened to be new was the rat problems. I was the only one who witnessed the rat problems after the other roommates left the apartment by force, one day of July 2018. That happened after I left court few days later. There will be more details about what happened to the rat on "the outcome of the court case" after this part.

The apartment was hollow and echoes when the roommates and I lived in it for almost a year. The apartment was hollower and echoes when it is empty. I was the only left in the apartment before I was forced out again at the end of October 2018. I was even afraid of my own shadow in the apartment. I want to go back one more time to what happened to the apartment across me. The landlord and management hired people and paid them very cheap to expose themselves on chemical dust, awful smells, and using chemical products without protection. I was not even protected since I had to expose myself to them to some degree, when I left and came back from work. The landlord and management also patch things up on the hallways and lobby. I mentioned on the previous book that the hallways and lobby was mess up while I came to look at the apartment and room with the broker. The building has been built since 1910's, and seems to never get maintenance since it has been built. All the landlord and management did after the incident that occurred was to hide problems. The apartment ended up renting out to other roommates, instead the roommates who were the victims of the incident. I wonder what happened to them after the incident occurred. I wonder if few, some, or all of them file lawsuit against the landlord and management, or they just forget about everything and moved on with their lives. These roommates happened to be Caucasians (probably two males and one female). The incident happened in a week or a week and half later, after all of us served by the landlord and management lawyer(s). The landlord, management, and their lawyer(s) described and labeled us as "dwellers" instead as "roommates". It seemed to be that we were living in the apartment illegally, free, while they collected money on rent from us. The other three roommates left one at a time at the end of April, beginning of May, and beginning of June of 2018. I even began to move most of my stuff out of the apartment that April and put them in the storage that does not have enough space to put things anymore. Despite the fact that we labeled as "dwellers", one of the roommates also labeled as "sub-landlord". I do not know if there was such thing as sub-landlord, as well as legalize in the housing system. Otherwise, it was just some people out there created their own things to control building(s). The reason why the landlord and management dropped all the responsibilities on that roommate was that she was in charge of the apartment. It was under that roommate which enabled the rest of us to move in the apartment. I wanted to say that the real estate and the broker who sent me to the apartment / room never told me anything about that.

I was not going to do anything until the court sent me paper or card, which I did not wait until the time that the landlord, management, and their lawyer(s) gave us expired for two reasons. The first reason was that one of the tenants, who lived in the building for almost a decade, told me I must go to court before the time expired. Otherwise I would be in trouble. The tenant was the only one who cared about what had been going in the building. The tenant told me that they offered him some money to leave the building and did not do so because the housing market is expensive and the money that they offered the tenant was not going to be helpful to the tenant. It seemed to be that the tenant may have been in the housing court before because the tenant told me that the court wants to do less. The tenant also added that he never sent response of any court cases to the opponent's lawyer because of privacy issue. The tenant did not want the other side to know about what he has on paper. The tenant was also aware of the ridiculous work that was going on in the building, after the incident that happened and about the cheap labor. The tenant also told me that I should send report to authority about everything, when I talked to him about I might do that. The second reason was that an employee, who works in the same company as me, told me that she was evicted without court date and trial. The employee added that the court did not care about anything, such as response on paper, but evicted anyone just like that. The employee just said that after the instructor of the class mentioned about the tenants are responsible to fix the apartments due to insurance issues. Therefore, I had no choice but to go to court a day before the date that the landlord, management, and their lawyer(s) gave me to comply to the amount that they claimed we owed expired. Despite the fact that I sent the same response to management and the law firm concerning about the charges were unfair and ridiculous which led to extortion, corruption, and robbery, along with the right zip code. I also warned the law firm and management about everything and the choice is theirs if they ignored what I sent to them. Therefore, the law firm turned out to be the primary target, as well as trapped the lawyers with their clients. I mentioned on the previous book about there is nothing sweeter than trapping a lawyer with his or her client, particularly when both of them are into funny business.

"I wonder if the insurance issue happens to be a new issue, or it has been there for a long time. I went to work one Sunday morning in place that I knew from my previous employer about four years ago, on December 2018. I found myself having some kind of "Seinfeld" episode in the basement or garage. Everywhere I went looked the same. I felt like a guinea pig trapped in the maze. It took me almost half an hour to get myself out through the gate that opened on the side of the building. The reason why I trapped in the basement was that I was looking for the place that the client had in the basement. I was looking for the data room to make sure everything was fine and scan barcodes as records. This time I got to stay at the lobby for my current employer. I spoke to the FSD who was there about the current and previous housing situations, as well as other issues. He was about early seventies, Caucasian. He was well knowledgeable about everything going on in housing court and other courts as well. He was aware that the Judges are like referees. I mentioned about the same thing in the previous book. He told me stories about that his whole family used to live in an apartment. His family gathered money to renovate the apartment. They spoke with the landlord about that. The landlord agreed. He told me that the landlord told him and his family that the apartment would stay the way it was when the landlord came to see the apartment after the renovation. I did not ask him whether or not the landlord told him and his family that the apartment was under their responsibilities to do private maintenance, even though they paid rent every month for maintenance. He also added that back in the days, Long-Island use to be a place people went there for summer vacation. He found it surprise that people spent a lot of money to stay there. He used a word that I never heard before to describe people are wasted their moneys on ridiculous houses."

I came to court and went on the second floor. I spoke with the Court Clerk about what would happen to me if the deadline that the landlord and the law firm gave me expired. The Court Clerk replied I would serve by the court for appearance. All I could say is that the Court Clerk did not collect my response due to the fact that it was not notarized. I did not know anything about notary. I wonder if this notary thing is new or not. The Court Clerk told me to take summon about I did not owe money on rent and told me to have my response collected on court date. The Court Clerk told me good luck which I did not need. I have everything at my disposal, as well as liability to go after the landlord, management, and the law firm. I did not send response to management and the law firm to warn them, but also trap them with the problem they have created. I knew people like them never listen when it comes to money. I would not be surprised if they ignored what I sent to them and did otherwise. They can be as unpredictable and impossible as they wanted in court. The previous cases I had to deal with taught me everything I needed to know, even though I have to deal with landlord instead of HDFC Co-Op. I focused on my part and objective. That is not my problem if the law firm and their clients got caught up into the abyss of their own problems and predicament. That is not also my problem if the court also contributed to the problems as well. The movie "The Rundown" by Dwayne Johnson was a great example. I sent my response to management and the law firm to tell them to walk out of the problems they created, or I will make them walked out of the problems they created. They wanted to test me. They thought they were clever. They wanted to know what I made off. Therefore, they chose the second choice, which turned out to be the wrong choice.

There are some issues that had been going on throughout the court case. The first issue had to do about serving me and other roommates to the wrong zip code on purpose. The second issue had to do about serving the other two roommates without their knowledge. The third issue had to do about the Proprietary Lease. The fourth issue had to do about the Stipulation of Agreement. The fifth issue had to do about the court did not collect my response and report I had at my disposal. The sixth issue had to do about there would not be audio records of what had been taken place in all court dates. The seventh issue had to do about illegal eviction without any protection, and kept sending me to places that would not do anything for me. There is something I want to say before I provide details about these issues. I wanted to say that I spent two nights at the shelter located on the east side in Manhattan. That was on the last week of May 2018. I went there for the first time in April 2018 to see if they could help me out. However, I went on the shelter located in Brooklyn, located around Nostrand Avenue area first. I had been told to check the shelter located on the east side of Manhattan, since the shelter in Brooklyn had been full.

The first person I spoke with after I spend about four hours or more of seating down, told me that action had not been taken against me yet. The first person told me that she placed me in the system for a year in case if anything happened. The first person I saw seemed to be nice and caring. The first person I saw told me that the shelter would find me a place to live without being specific whether if it was an apartment or a room (roommates). I went to the shelter right after work that day after spending nearly seven hours in the shelter. However, thing changed when I came back to the shelter on late night of May 30, 2018, at around 7pm. The second person I saw that night seemed to have some issues to deal with and wondered what type of issues. The second person wanted to do was to ignore and careless about my problems, by making things easy for herself. The second person did not want to report about what I said to her on the previous case and current case. The second person wanted to report a different case other than the actual ones that occurred to me. Therefore, I will be held responsible and accountable of something I had been forced to say as false statement. I was under suspicion that she may be incapable to report and had no understanding of the complexity of what I had been through. The second person even told me that I could not afford to pay for an apartment because of my income. The second person told me that the only option for me was to rent a room. It took me about six hours or more just to get a room temporally for the night. I got the room around 1am, on May 31, 2018.

I found that so strange that the shelter got involved into this roommate thing. I tried to avoid and escape it. The system forced me right into it. The public and private would never want to be held responsible and accountable when I will come back in court over the issues of false charges that would be done under corruption, extortion, and robbery again. The court would be careless if I would come back to court over the same issues again. I wanted to say that one of the Judges accused unfairly and unjustly by saying that I got myself into the mess that I was in. I wondered if the court accused me based on free will or desperation. Therefore, it was the desperation act got me into the mess. The court had to prove to me if I got myself into the mess based on my free will. The first book had details about everything that happened to me. I reached out to the court, but no one came to my rescue. Therefore, the court had left me neglected and abandoned. I met with another lady the same day after work. I had been told to see her at certain time; otherwise I would lose the opportunity. That was what the second person told me before I went to the room that night. The second person gave me the paper that had appointment on it. I met with the other lady and she showed me some rooms that were available. The rooms that she showed was about $800 or $850 and higher per month. The lady told me that was all she could find for me. She told me that to go to court and found out about the Judge's decision and brought the marshal eviction paper with me. She added that I was not evicted yet. She added that to call her if I got evicted so that I would not be affected by the shelter rules and regulations which I knew about them because I used to work in a family shelter for almost six months. The lady helped me found another room temporally for the second night. There are some details about the condition of the shelter on the "outcome of the court case".

I forgot whether the first person or the second person told me that I was not homeless for the last past four years because I lived in somebody else house. I found it so strange and absurd of the shelter told me that I was not homeless in the last past four years. I remembered I took a class in college that I was not prepared to take on my first spring semester. I had to drop the class due to the lack of my poor writing skills I needed to work on. I did understand what was going on in class, and everything captured my attention. I also had to drop the class because I was not prepared for the assignments and exams. The professor said in class one day that there were two types of homelessness. The first type of homelessness was the one that was visible. The professor meant to refer to the people who are sleeping on the streets. The second type of homelessness was the one that was invisible and did not count as homelessness. The professor meant to refer to the people who are living in others' houses. Therefore, it is quite evident that the second type of homelessness is much higher than the first type of homelessness. No wonder why the landlord and the law firm labeled us as dwellers; being roommates are associated with dwellers which leading to homelessness. Therefore the landlord and law firm accused us of leaving in the apartment illegally, even though the landlord and management collected money on rent from us every month. The shelter should know about the second type of homelessness, otherwise they are in denial of it. It would be absurd of them to say that they did not know about the second type of homelessness, as well as saying there is no such thing. The word dwellers must have been use to certain people due to their racial backgrounds instead of everyone labels like that regardless their racial backgrounds.

I wonder what had been going on in "John Doe and Jane Doe" cases in the court room next to the one that I had been on the fourth floor. It seemed to be that "John Doe and Jane Doe" cases are common cases in housing court because it happens in all courtrooms on very floor to higher extent, when I checked the floors at the end of October 2019 for two days while on vacation. There were more than four cases like that happened in the courtroom next door almost every time I came to court. I had to deal with a case like that in 2014 (stipulation of agreement). I wonder if the outcome of the cases were the same as mine or not. I wonder if the "John Doe and Jane Doe" falls in the same category as the second type of homelessness. The second type of homelessness is that the people who face it are living illegally in strangers, friends, roommates, and family houses. Therefore, I am living illegally in my uncle's apartment after the eviction took place at the end of October 2018, to escape living with roommates and found myself going back to court for more than six times for no reason at all. I mentioned on my previous book about my uncle's apartment was better than the one I evicted from under identity theft, perjury, falsify information and documents on purpose in 2014. However, my uncle's apartment is worst just like the one I evicted from illegally in 2014. My uncle's apartment was not in the state that it was when I came to New York over twenty years ago, and ten years ago which was the last time I went to my uncle's apartment to help him with something. My uncle decided to put carpets on the floor of the apartment (living room and bedroom) because some of the woods began to get really loose. My uncle also decided to put tiles in the hallway of the apartment. I can still feel some of the woods moving under my feet while walking, along with the squeaky sound. The apartment is hollow and echoes as well. Any light objects that drops on the floor of the apartment make sound or noise. The floor of the apartment and the one's above him are under the same condition. The person above my uncle did make huge noises. My uncle ended up got angry about that which makes him very unhappy. However, his unhappiness of the noises that happened from the apartment above him may not be the only causes of his unhappiness. I pay so much attention to human being. The old telling says keep your friend close, and your enemy closer. As for me, I keep everything closest to me. His unhappiness of the noises going on from the apartment above is mixed up with other unhappiness. I already told him that the police and the court would never do about his problem, as well as the law. I advised him not to keep going to court unprepared. I met with my uncle in court in 2013. He explained the issue he had to deal with in the apartment. He told me that he stopped paying rent and kept all of the payments to have the landlord to come to fix the apartment. My uncle even showed me all the money orders. However, we were not in the same courtroom at that time. Therefore, the apartment remained without maintenance and my uncle told me that he was forced to pay for the rents. They sent people to do some painting and concealed holes he had on the ceiling of his bedroom in the middle of year 2018. My uncle even told me that mice caused the holes on the ceiling of his bedroom. He added that he saw mice falling down from the ceiling from one of the holes sometimes. Someone came one weekend of July 2018 to check on the lousy work. I did the best I can to explain to the person about the housing problem that all landlords know the problems that happened in the apartments. The person tried to avoid me and talk to my uncle when he found out my uncle happened to be vulnerable due to language barrier politically and socially.

"Speaking of noise, I suffered more on that heavily around the years 2010 until the illegal eviction took place in 2014 from the couples who lived above us illegally in May 2008. The sexual intercourse got louder below me more likely at night. Sometime I woke up in the middle of the night to use restroom and heard it. The couples made loud voice while they argue. The woman toasted the chair at the man and made gunshot sounds type. I witnessed them argue like that twice. I was under suspicious that the lady may have had

caught her man cheated. The lady apologized to us in a note that she left at our apartment's door. The lady did not apologize in any way at all the second time. I wonder how many times the couple had been argued while we were not in the apartment. I could hear them walking all day and night above us. It would awkward of me to call police to report to them about sexual activities that took place above me. It would be awkward of me to either pick up a broom to poke the ceiling, or went to knock on their door to tell them they were loud with their sexual activities. The couples above me even listen to music in high volume, watching and playing games in loud speakers. The other issues concerning about the apartment above me is on the previous book. As for the place I evicted recently was that it was louder in the neighborhood all day and all night. I could say that so much noise going on and I could barely hear the long island train running. The music blast off from cars and the restaurant below of the building. There was a place across the street on the other side of the building has parties and sometimes fight broke out on the street and hoping that no one pulled out guns and started to shoot. I still manage to sleep at night in both apartments despite all of these noise problems."

I remembered my uncle told me that the court gave him a lawyer for one of his cases. One day the lawyer called him and intended to charge him over one thousand dollars for represented him. My uncle told me that he cursed him over the phone and hung up. I wondered if the lawyer happened to be the one who prevented my uncle's apartment from getting maintenance, due to the lack of lawyer's fees. My uncle even told me that the lawyer did not do anything at all to help solve his housing problem. My uncle told me that as a senior, the landlord should not raise the rent on him. My uncle added that there is a law prohibited that from happening. I did not say anything because my uncle will not listen to what I had to say. I just listen to him and remained quiet. The landlord does not care about the law that never inforce by the court because the landlord would never raise the rent on my uncle when the landlord knows that he or she would get in deep trouble when the court tells him or her not to. Otherwise, one has to bring proof of a lawsuit against rent hikes on seniors when landlords turn out to be stubborn by ignoring the law. I want to know how much the lawsuit would be on that.

I even let my uncle knew that I am in his apartment illegally and I will get evicted if anything happened. Therefore "John Doe and Jane Doe" is one of the strategies, or the only strategy to make that happened. If some lawyers try effectively saying that I could not represent my parents in court in 2013 (second HP action case); the same would apply there towards my uncle. Therefore, I kept using the P.O Box to receive my mail. I was glad that I did not close the P.O. Box when I moved in the apartment or room in 2017 as roommate when I found out there was no guaranty of staying for a long term, or permanently. I would go through exactly the same thing from the previous and current cases that the court would never provide me with protection. Therefore I would find myself back on the streets again. I hope that I find something or place quickly because my days are numbered again. It is difficult to tell people who are not aware what happened around them and they never listen to what you try to tell them. That happened because not only of their stubbornness, but also they do not listen to people who are much younger than them. They still want to control everything when they keep adding to the problems. They think they know everything when they are actually not. Therefore, I will inherit my uncle's problem, just like I did for my father's problem. I would end up doing the same type work I do in this current book and, particularly the previous book. I hope that my uncle does what is right to minimize in the problem. I hope that my uncle does not do what my father did without any protection for himself and us. Since I find out my uncle has a lawyer, which could complicate things more because I do not know what he did before and could complicate things in the future.

I begin to find out that people with property could cause serious harm to their families if they do not do what is right. However, property issues could cause problem, as well as complicated things in court. I saw few cases like that in court and I witnessed one issue in November 2018 that I gave details about after the issues' parts. I could say that one has to be strong and knowledgeable politically and socially in order to deal with the housing situation in court effectively. Otherwise, one would lose his or her property if he or she is unable to be politically and socially strong and knowledgeable. I find it sad when I see people are raising their children in this life without knowing what is really going on around. They end up saying that it is hard for them and barely have time to deal with other things, like their jobs or their careers. I can say that having children and careers in this life are enormous responsibly, but the least. The political, social, and economics live we are living are also enormous on both national and international level. They are part of our core survival in life. Above all they are our responsibilities collectively and individually. Therefore, we are responsible to fulfill them every day regardless our class, race, and gender differences. Therefore, we have to fulfill them even though we do not have time.

There was a book that someone at work gave me in summer 2018 and I had been told to read it twice which I did last time in 2019. The title of the book is "Falun Gong" (by Li Hongzhi). The book is useful because there are a lot going on in it. There are things that the author talked about which I have awareness about a long time ago. There are things that the author talked about is also new for me, beside the spiritual aspect of the practice. As an Asian author, we are not so different after all to talk about the common problems and issues that everyone faced in the world in our personal life and in life over all. I know that the spiritual aspect of the book may be hard for some people to understand and accept it, but the other aspects of the book are easy and straight forward for all of us to understand and accept it. The biggest problems that some human beings continue to suffer from are the strong attachment they have with sex, power, and money. Those problems turn out be deadly drugs for some human beings. The author of the book "confession of an economic hitman" talks about those deadly drugs in his book and on radio station. No one with these types of attachments would give them up to save world. They would never lower their attachments on them to bring relief to the world. I saw and witnessed that twice on other issues that had to do with other gains. The outcome of them nearly the same because few of those who were there that day said they do not care about the what happened in other countries, as long as they get what they want from those countries. I will not be specific about where they happened, but were shocked of the responses from those who said it. Therefore, some people could not make some simple sacrifice to help save the world, or bring relief to the world.

The author also talks about not to feel angry when some people curse you and give you hard time because it is not worth it to do the same. There are more to what the author said by going beyond it. I began to see that problem twenty years ago and it is not worth it to waste my time with some people who are disrespected me because they do not have respect for themselves, and try to bring me down to their levels. I have been disrespected by people who are oldest, older, and younger than me regardless their genders. The previous court cases were the proof that. Some people have their own purpose on that so that they can start some trouble for no reason at all, but wonder if they want to hurt someone or kill someone, and ended up acting as the victims or innocents. The way things are in the world at this moment that some people are jobless, wondering they kind of thoughts going on in their mind to attack anyone who do not pause problem and threat to them. I witnessed some people went through that and I experienced that one day of summer 2018 while I took a quick break to go buy something at the seven elven store located closer where I work. This trouble man, African American probably in his mid-twenties, did two worst things to me. The first thing was that I was behind him, about three feet behind him. He had the guts and nerve to tell to keep moving back which I did not. The second thing was that he used what appeared to be credit cards and knowing for sure that his card was declined. I did not say anything or even smile. He threatened me by saying that he was about to throw the coffee on my face, if I thought that he could not pay for the coffee. Therefore, he could not buy the coffee because he did not have money on him. The gentleman who was at the register decided to him the coffee for free which that was what he wanted to begin with. I began to find out that despite the fact that one has respect toward everyone, does not mean that he or she would get respect back from everyone. I find out that the more one has respect for himself or herself the better. Respect is not some kind of commodity that some of us tend to trade. I saw and witnessed some people intend to disrespect those who do not show them respect. Some people even accused others disrespect them when they are not. Otherwise, they want to sue those they accuse of disrespect them. Respect is the basic needs of all human beings in this world since the beginning of time.

There was another book I just finished reading recently. The title of the book is "Solve for happy" (by Mo Gawdat). Someone else advised me to read the book. The title of the book also captures my attention. I was glad I read the book because the author of the book explained a lot about how ones could find happiness in life despite all of the other problems, issues, and hardship that we all face in this life, in the world, and in our personal life. There are a lot of things that I have in common with the author, particularly when it comes to certain movies and sitcom. I remember one of the classes I took a year before graduation had a small discussion about how one could be happy and angry at the same time. Therefore, that leads to contradiction. One has to choose one of them, not both of them. After, what I have been through for the last past five years, I do not know whether I should be mad or happy. I knew and everyone should know that being in anger also affect the body physically and mentally, particularly mentally which could also raise the risk of getting sick severely. I wonder how others would feel if they have been in the same situation that I have been in the last past six years heavily. Let's get back to the housing court issues.

When a tenant brings a landlord to court, the tenant faces punishment of not having his or her apartment receives maintenance. The landlord would not be happy to have the tenant bring him or her in court when the landlord uses the finance of the building to fund his or her lawyer, and all of the tenants in the building would pay for that on rent hikes permanently. When the tenant has the guts and courage to go after the landlord and the landlord's lawyer(s), the punishment for the tenant is illegal eviction without protection; even though the tenant lives more than ten, fifteen, and thirty years in the apartment. Therefore, that is what my uncle and others who bring the landlords in court and unable to fight for themselves, faced the punishment of not having their apartments receiving maintenance. People like this may fail to pay attention that going to court is expensive, particularly when cases going on trials. The court and the law firms would never tell the accurate estimation or total cost for court cases. The current court case I had to deal with was already exceeding twenty thousand dollars owed by whom. I will find it absurd of the court to tell me that I owed money that there was no proof of owing, and yet I do not have or possess this type of cash. Otherwise the court would be an accessory to extortion, corruption, and robbery that the landlord committed toward me. As I mentioned before that I was into this mess because of the court. Therefore, the court has to pick up the tab. The previous court cases remain totally uncertain about the whole amount. The current court case is already enormous. The previous court cases are far more enormous. Therefore, I hope in the future to find out about both current and previous court cases. I want to say that I do not blame the tenants when they file for HP action against the landlords, Co-Ops, and City agency for maintenance. These tenants would get blame by the same system which does not want to do anything at all about the problem as the victims. It will be easier for the system to blame these tenants for not doing anything. Otherwise, some of these tenants have to take matters into their own hands which turn them out to be the sacrificial lambs to deal with the mess and all of the problems that come along with the mess. I happen to be the sacrificial lamb to deal with not only with the housing situations, but also other problems as well. I wonder who would pay me for all of the work that I have been done, particularly being my own representative, investigator, and reporter. I live in a capitalistic society, and who is going to pay me for doing all of these works. Otherwise, I feel that I work for free when I do not live in communist society. Otherwise, both systems are the same just like a coin. I wonder which one of them is the head or the tail. Otherwise, it does not matter which one is. Otherwise, I may be mistaken of what I said.

I watched the movie "Molly's game", by Jessica Chastain and Idris Elba, which based on true story. The lawyer charged her over one hundred thousand dollars of attorney's fees to represent her in court (maybe for the offenses, and no rewards). I wonder if she had to pay the full fees since the lawyer did not say a word in court. The judge called the other side and decided to close the case after reviewing the court case. The judge found out that the crime that she committed was not necessarily big crime of open indoors casino and about six million dollars or more owed to her by players, and her life had been threaten on top of that by the mobs. The Judge simply gave her few hours of community service and found out that there more major financial crimes that happened in the country, affecting the country and the world to profound ways, and those who committed the crime went unpunished. It would be unfair to convict and prosecute her of a crime that has no major or minor financial crime in the country and the world. I wonder if she had to pay the lawyer the whole fees or a small percentage of the fee for preparing the court case. I wonder how much that small fees would be. I also wonder if a person of color, whether male or female would get the same treatment of something that appeared to be a minor crime, regardless of the type of class that color person is living in, for the same condition. That is really hard to tell, unless we get there to find out about that.

Let's get back to the housing issues. All of the housing cases that have been, always ended to major offenses. Those offenses run at their deepest level. The lawyers who cause those major offenses seem to go unpunished by the system. They should have had their licenses revoke for committing those offenses. Otherwise, some lawyers got away with crimes and punishment not only under right, power, and privilege, but also due to racial preference and favoritism. I have to do all of the workload to go after these lawyers and their clients. Otherwise, the court asks them to pay fees for those major offenses and wonder how much for the fees. I began to find out some lawyers can take a major crime and turn it into a small crime and vice versa. One can only tell when one reads all the ridiculousness they put on paper when the paper full of problems, contradiction, omitting, and lies. There was story I watch either 20/20 or 60 minutes one Sunday afternoon, about a woman who was raped by a Caucasian male. The case went on trial and the male only get about six months or less in jail. The victim found that unfair because the defendant should suffered severely for a major crime like this. I wonder that happened due to the reason that the victim is an Asian female. She even said that a black person would get more than four years in jail for having marijuana in his pocket. It was strange that the court allowed the defendant's lawyer to have the court case fitted his narrative, instead of taking the facts into account and consideration. The lady even published a book about what happened and how the court system was unfair to her. I could say that the lady was lucky that she was not pregnant. It could have had been a major issue for her is was pregnant and wanted to have an abortion due to unwanted pregnancy. Some people from politics, social, and religious would interfere to go against her free will, and none of them would take full responsibility when this child growing up to become a problem for society. They would blame her for something that she tried to avoid of having to begin with. I began to find out in that there are some situations should have never being part of political, social, and religious, when they are personal matters that do not any relations to them. As for the housing court case, I was lucky enough on the current court case that I kept my personal record in case of something like that might happen. Lawyers like that think they clever and their cleverness can use against them when someone actually goes after them and their clients. The law firm paper or document is based on their narrative, while they left behind, excluded, or omitted all the major offenses and wrongdoings that the lawyers had been committed throughout the court cases. It had happened before on the previous housing count cases (HP action 2013 and Holdover Proceeding 2014). Therefore, this is another "déjà vu" I experience all over again. That problem is not my problem, but the court's problem because the court allows lawyers to do that.

The First Issue

Serving to the wrong zip code on purpose

The law firm and the landlord knew for fact that they use wrong zip code on purpose. They both did that on purpose so that we could come in court late and miss the opportunity to represent ourselves in court on time. Everything that the law firm and their clients sent to the wrong zip code, will be received to the right zip code almost a week later from the date that the letters or documents sent to us. Despite the fact that I sent response to the law firm with the right zip code, the law firm kept going along with the wrong zip code into the court case. The Court and the Marshal used the same wrongful zip code because they kept things the way the landlord and the law firm had on file from the beginning. One of the Judges said that it was not perjury to serve someone to the wrong zip code on purpose in other words. I brought it to the court's attention whether or not the court aware or ignore it, after the eviction took place while I was out of town.

Another problem within the first issue is that the law firm and their client brought all of us in court, but trying to dump the responsibility to one of us. I mentioned about the girl was the one who came first in the apartment, happened to be the sub-landlord. I also mentioned that I never knew if there was such thing as sub-landlord. Otherwise it was just some people out there creating their own laws, rules, and regulations without approval from the Authorities. The law firm, their clients, and the court knew that the girl left and she had been brought in court without her knowledge. I found it absurd and trickery of the law firm told me twice that I should not be in court. My name and the other roommate names were on the law firm record and the court record to show up in court. The law firm tried to trick me to leave the court and used that against me to have the court ruled over me unfairly on purpose, which would lead to unfair eviction. The law firm would deny anything about that. The court never asked me about what had been discussed out of the courtroom before facing the Judge. I wonder who knew how many people evicted like that in the city serving on the wrong zip code on purpose. Therefore, I would be the scapegoat (or patsy) out of everything. I have been used as scapegoat (or patsy) by the lawyer who stole my $17000 in 2014 as I mentioned before. The lawyer blamed and accused me of trying to vacate the Judge decision when I asked him my money back with few percentages off the whole amount.

I remembered there were two young married couples ended up in the family shelter I used to work early 2013. One day they told me that they were evicted illegally without any court date. The couples told me that they were rented space from somebody. The person never told them that he was in court. The person bailed out before the eviction took place. Therefore, they were the one who suffered the consequence of everything. The couples told me that the eviction happened due to failure of rent payments. The couples told me that they pay rent to the person. Their names never appeared in court that they were sharing space with the person. That was the same thing that the board and their lawyer(s) did to us on the Holdover Proceeding case. They both knew about my father's absence and they ended up doing things under his name. They excluded me and my mother out of everything. They used fake names to bring me and my father in court. That was the reason why they use "John Doe and Jane Doe" as an excuse, advantage, and pretext on purpose to commit wrongdoings. They ended up using my first name as my last name, and misspelling my father's first name on purpose to commit perjury, falsify information and documents, and Identity theft. The court would have ruled over me and my father if I did not show up in court. I would eventually get evicted without trial. I wonder how many more tricks these lawyers and their clients could come up with to evict tenants out of their apartments. That happened because there are flaws and loopholes in the housing court. The tenants have been left on their own to figure them out on their court cases.

I wonder how the court case would be if all four of us happened to show up in court. The collectivism and individualism might be an issue there. What if half of us decided not to pay the whole amount that the law firm and their clients stated that we owed on purpose? What if I was the only one decided not to pay the whole amount that the law firm and their client stated that we owe on purpose? Therefore, the lawyers would have created confusion out of the case and forced me to pay. The lawyers would use the others as their advantage to make me pay the whole amount by force. That was what happened with us since we moved in the apartment. The others ended up paying the amount that management claimed that they owed, which they did not owe. We reached out to the real estate that brought us to the apartment. Therefore, the real estate did not do anything to help out. I was the only one who did not pay over two hundred dollars that management claimed that I owed. They added up about fifty dollars every ten days to that amount. It was absurd for them to charge me for few days I did not spent in the apartment. I warned management about what they did led to corruption, extortion, and robbery in 2017. I paid $775 on deposit and $775 for monthly rent (mid-May to end of June). The paper or the record that real estate gave me had the information about the date I should move in the apartment or room was in June 1, 2017. Therefore, this was one of the evidence that the court almost not collected from me in August 2018. Therefore, that amount including to the two months owed by one roommate, exceeding more than four thousand dollars and adding the lawyer's fees. The whole amount exceeded more than twenty dollars at the end of the court date. I have been told to pay more than eleven thousand dollars on fees that I did not owe, and took responsibility of over three thousand dollars on monthly rent. I have been responsible for the whole amount of the rent since I happened to be the one left behind with the responsibilities. Therefore, all of these amounts had been done on the wrong zip code on purpose and wondered why. The court should pay that amount since I have been into this mess because of the court as I mentioned before. That also proves that I have not been served properly on purpose over the zip code problem and issue which done on purpose.

The Second Issue

Serving the others without their knowledge

I found it strange that it is right, fair, and just to bring someone in court without his or her knowledge. The landlord and management tried to be clever (sneaky, slicky, and sleazy). They forced us out on May 31, 2018 and yet began to serve us on the middle of May by their lawyers on the wrong zip code on purpose. The landlord and management seemed to never report to their lawyers about the deadline that they gave us to leave the apartment. Otherwise, the lawyers may have known about the deadline, but pretended not to know about it. I brought everything to the court's attention, and the law firm knew about the others absence, including the dates of their absences. However, the first two roommates did not know about they had been served without their knowledge. The other one did know about it, but already decided to move out when he found out that everything was too much for him to handle. I want to say that all of the roommates aware the response I sent to management by email because I sent the email to them as well.

I do not blame the other roommates that they leave because how would they be able to handle themselves in court regardless some, few, and all of them might be college graduates. As I mentioned in my previous book that it does not matter if a person knows how to read and write, but knowing how to deal with them in court is another matter (including every other matters, issues, problems, and conflicts one has to deal with in life as a whole). I mentioned earlier about not being residence of the New York City, and wondered how the court case would be handled over such issue. Otherwise, there is no problem on that at all. I also did not know if the others had the intention of renewing the lease or not. I was the only tried to renew the lease twice, but rejected and denied by management over the form that send to us by email and mail. That happened because management wanted us to pay the whole amount owed under corruption, extortion, and robbery. Otherwise, we all have to leave. I wonder who wants to pay for somebody else debt. Management claimed that it had been stated on the lease that all roommates held responsible and accountable for the debt done by other roommates.

I also wonder how the law firm would deal with the problem of all of us being in court. I wonder if the law firm would charge the landlord and management per person, or one full fee, and how much that fee would be per court date. Otherwise, it may have had happened already because all of us were already on the court record to show up. The law firm would charge the landlord and management for the others even though they did not show up in court at all. Therefore, the tenants of the building would pick up the debt of the landlord and management, since they used the building finance to bring us and many more in court to commit corruption, extortion, and robbery. I do not think that we were the only one that the landlord and management brought in court over wrongful charges. One tenant and one roommate who just moved in the building during the time I was in court with the landlord and management, told me about wrongful charges. I asked the roommates while I saw her came in the building. She told me that they charged her and the others on the wrongful charges. There was a part like that on the previous book about that some tenants told me that they had been charged wrongfully by their landlords. I wondered how their court issues handled in court because those wrongful charges were being done on purpose by landlords to commit corruption, extortion, and robbery just to maximize profit and passed the lawyers' bill on the tenants. The only way for the landlords to do so, is to raise the rent to higher rates. Those wrongful charges problems and issues happened to be common cases in housing court.

The Third Issue

Proprietary Lease Dilemma

The Proprietary Lease was one of the major issues, not in court only, but also on the day I made the transaction to get the room. The real estate which helped me found the room, told me to sign papers, but never told me anything about lease; as well as the terms and conditions contain on the lease. I also wonder if those terms and conditions were going to be on my favor or the landlord's and management's favor. Therefore, I would effectively force myself to accept and agree into something that is unfair, unjust, and vice. I also wonder how the lease issue would have handled in court if there was evidence that I agreed with those terms and conditions on the lease.

However, that was what the law firm and their clients tried to do was to force themselves aggressively on the lease under trickery. The landlord and his lawyer(s) came in court with the copy of the documents that the roommates and I signed with different dates on the documents; and stapled the documents behind the lease to make it look like I accepted the terms and conditions. I witnessed about that behind closed door on August 2018. One of the roommates who left the apartment last, told me there was a lease. I told him that I never received any lease on the day I got the room from the real estate. I was already in court with the landlord and management, and it was too late for that. On the first day of court (June 2018), I witnessed behind closed door about the discussion over the lease. I had been told that I should held responsible and accountable to pay for money that I did not owe, as well as held responsible and accountable to pay full amount of rent for the empty rooms. I had been told by the gentleman who represented and worked for the court or Judge and the first lawyer who presented which one of the landlord's phony organizations. They both told me it was lawful and constitutional about what the landlord and management had on the lease when I asked them if everything that they told me are lawful and constitutional. Therefore that was why I had to update my report on that problem and issue. There are more details about everything on that report.

The lease in that case reminded me of the unfair, unjust, wrongful laws, and constitution of slavery. The slave masters used the government to keep the slave in bondage by using the laws and constitution as fair, right, virtue, legal, and just. The slave masters used the laws and constitution in order to commit murder, rape, unpaid labor, and severely punishment of the slaves. The slave masters used the Government to maximize their profits at the back of the slaves. Therefore, the country had committed the worse human right violation in history than what happened during world war two. The world could never give the truth about everything that happened during world war two. The media always gives medium or less than medium out of every serious event that happened in world histories. One has to go the other way around to get deep reasons and truth why every major event occurred, because the media would never told them nothing but simply bias, lame, and nonsense stories to hide the truth from everyone. I always say that it is painful enough to have the innocent blood of my brothers, sisters, or my countrymen. It is more painful to have somebody else's innocent blood other than my brothers, sisters, or countrymen, particularly when they are far away and not being my neighbors.

Therefore, it is quite evident to say that landlords create lease like that turned out to be slave masters to their tenants. One should know by now that landlord means master of the land and master of everyone who live on the land. It is the monarchy and capitalist system (including other few systems which omitted here) used as combination or in unity there. That is why the law firm and their clients got the guts and nerve to force me to pay money that I did not owe. They did so by using economic gangsters, and mafia to commit corruption, extortion, and robbery. The law firm and management tried to use the court system as advantage to make me pay money that I did not owe. The landlord and management used the finance of the building to fund or hire lawyers, and used the lawyers as economic hitman to make me pay money I did not owe. The court and the law firm know that the tenants would pay the expense under rent hikes with high interest. It seemed to be that it has been stated in all proprietary lease that tenants should pay the lawyer expenses event though they are innocent of everything.

I can see the reason why the board on the previous case turned the Co-Op into landlord (2013-2014). They did so because they want to become slave masters of the shareholders. The president that no one voted for, testified by saying that HDFC is the landlord. I have the audio record as a proof. The president knew what he was doing. He and the others went out of their own to act as landlords in the Co-Op because the find out that they could get right, power, privilege, and wealth out of landlorship. That was also the reason why the president and the others went on proprietary lease and ignored the fake Bylaws that he and the others gave me, after they found out that their lawyers and them trapped with the fake Bylaws. I do not think proprietary lease had it used in the HDFC Co-Op when the Bylaws was the only thing that the building needed. The TIL only included the Bylaws, not lease. It is absurd to have lease for something that I bought and owned. Therefore, the president and the others knew what they had been doing and done so on purpose. The law firms which help them happened to be accessory to the criminal activities their clients had committed. The same thing is applied to the current case because the law firm happened to be accessory to crimes that their clients had committed. We all have been harassed by the landlord and management to pay fees that we do not owe, even though the others compelled themselves to pay few of those illegal fees. Therefore, I make the independent choice myself not to pay for something that I do not owe. I began to find out that when one gives into one thing, he or she give in to everything else. That is the whole package. Therefore that is the problem with right, freedom, and democracy because they could be used on the negative manners and matters. That is also problem with collectivism when people submitted themselves to wrong things, affected others who do not want to be part of the wrong things.

The fourth Issue

The stipulation of agreement dilemma

There was something strange happened when I came back to court on the second time. The court should have had dismissed, close, or withdraw the case, and did not do so. There was something interesting I want to say before I faced the Judge in about few minutes later, on the second trip in court. It was about a case before me. The landlord's lawyer wanted to evict a female tenant who was about seventy years of age, African-American, due to unfair rent hikes or unfair charges by the landlord. The Judge stopped the lawyer and told the lawyer that would not happened because the tenant was a retire veteran who served the country for years. The Judge helped the tenant and guide the tenant on how to pay the rent, provided the tenant extra information about where to go to get help. I saw few cases almost like that held by the two courtrooms that I had been, particularly in August 2018, where lawyers forced the Judges to evict tenants illegally. The Judge had no choice but to protect those vulnerable tenants against wrongdoings. However, that does not mean that these tenants would not face eviction after the court decisions stated not to do so. It was up to the landlords and their lawyers to go against the judges' decisions to evict tenants illegally. Therefore, there is no guarantee by the court that the tenants are protected from illegal eviction. The current case and previous case I had to deal with turned out to be like that. I have been evicted illegally without the court protection twice.

The lawyer left and came back few minutes later, after the Judge made the decision on the court case about preventing the eviction took place. The lawyer asked the gentleman who handled the case files for "application" on our court case. I knew that because the lawyer gave the case number that was stated on the list, not the index number. I was lucky enough to keep my eyes and ears opened to hear and see what the lawyer said. I was also lucky enough to seat not far away where the court files had been held. The gentleman told the lawyer to ask the Judge for permission on that. Therefore, the lawyer trapped with everything. However, this is not the first time that lawyers asked for application on court case. It was like a "déjà vu" to me. The lawyer who represented the Co-Op asked for application on the small claimed I filed against the Co-Op, particularly against the head or chief officer of the Co-Op in 2013. I warned the law firm to stay away from their clients on the response that I sent to the law firm on the HP action case and the small claim case in 2013. The law firm though that they could come and mess things up, particularly made things worse and not taken responsibility, as well as not held accountable for anything. Therefore, the application was the first plan for the lawyer trying to escape or avoid the court case.

The lawyer called out the sub-landlord's name (name omitted for the purpose of the book, the first roommate), and I happened to be the one to stand up. I could care less about what the lawyer had to say anyway because the law firm ignored the response I sent, and I would not allow the lawyer to get to me. I asked the lawyer what happened to the first lawyer that came in court last time. The second lawyer responded that there was no problem on that, and he was the one handled the case now. It was like I had another "déjà vu" all over again. This was not the first time that lawyers change for the same court case without my knowledge and the court's knowledge. That happened because the law firm trapped with the court case with their clients. The reason why lawyers change for the same court case was that the lawyers tried to undo their mess that was impossible to undo. Otherwise, pretense and excuse are the only options available for them to deny everything I send to them. That was not my business if the first lawyer did not report to the second lawyer of what happened in court on the first trip in court. That was what happened before and during the trial of the second HP action case in 2013. That was what happened after the trial of the holdover proceeding in 2014. The same lawyers and their law firms knew about everything and they still committed wrongdoings towards me anyway. The same thing applied to the current case.

That was not the first time lawyers call me out of the courtroom, just tried to force me out of the court cases by fear. The lawyers, particularly the second lawyer, called me out of the courtroom as the second plan. I had another "déjà vu" there as well. The first time that happened was on the second HP action case in 2013. I thought that lawyers only done that on paper. The second time that happened was from the same lawyer on the Holdover Proceeding case in 2014. The lawyer called me out of the court room in few minutes before I had date for the trial of the Holdover Proceeding in 2014. The lawyer did not use paper this time. The lawyer tried to use fear and intimidation as a weapon to make sure I did not go through with everything. However, in this current court case, the two lawyers use different strategy which turned out to be the same type. I mentioned earlier about that lawyers tried to trick me not show up, even though my name was on the court record to show up. It was absurd of the second lawyer to tell me not to show up, and may had been under pretense that the first lawyer did not tell them about what happened on the first trip in court. Therefore, both lawyers knew that they brought the other two roommates in court without their knowledge. Therefore, the second plan to get out of the court case had been ruined for them. It was also absurd for a lawyer to take on case from another lawyer without knowing what happened previously and picked up from there. Therefore, this was the only beginning of moving backward on purpose to the court case, while the court case was moving forward. That was also another "déjà vu" I experienced there on backwardness. I witnessed that happened on the second HP action case (2013) and the Holdover Proceeding case (2014).

The court case got stranger and weirder when the lawyer came to the Judge and stated that the landlord was unable to make it due to the Jewish holiday. I wondered if every month considers as Jewish holiday. It is evident that some people are continue to use religion as an excuse, advantage, and/or pretext to get away with wrongdoings. Some people use religion as tools to commit slavery. Some people use religion as tools to force teenage girls into marriage with older adults. There was an episode of a television series was about that issue. The television series also gave an ideal solution how to deal with the problem not to blame the victims when the victims are retaliated against force marriage for may be economic purpose and force into sexual intercourse, get pregnant, and more chance to give birth to premature babies. Some people use religion as tools to commit rape. There was a case like that held in court at end of the year 2018 where the defendant may have go free of raping a girl due to the law stated on the bible. Therefore, there is a thin line of between rape that is legal and illegal. Some are continued to use religion as tools to establish their political, social, and economic interest, as well as, power, privilege, right, and value.

However, this is another "déjà vu" I have to deal with to some degree there. The first lawyer, who represented the board on the second HP action case in 2013, did that. The lawyer said to the court that he was unable to show up in court on Jewish holiday which pushed the court case to two months instead of one month. Otherwise, the lawyer and his clients (the board) just want to buy themselves more time and wasted mine on purpose. I found it unfair of the Judge did not ask me if I was fine with that. It was as if I was not existed at all. All I could see from the Judge was a little fear as if the court would get in trouble if the court does not obey Jewish holiday. It is fine for the lawyer to go to marshal to evict me on Jewish holiday after he and his clients went against the Judge decision on the Holdover Proceeding case in 2014. This time I had to do something about that. I am getting sick and tired of people who are in charge and being irresponsible. The response I gave is on the "outcome of the court case". I would find it unfair, prejudice, discrimination, and injustice if I have been accused of anti-semantic. Therefore, some people use religion as an excuse, advantage, and/or pretext not to show up in court. I saw some Jewish people came to court on the Jewish holiday later on. Does that mean that they are not religious? The landlord should have been in court since day one, but did not show up on purpose. The gentleman who worked for the court told the first lawyer that the landlord must show up on the next court date which supposed to be trial. The landlord and management change lawyers, and the law firm knew and aware what is going in court. The law firm and their clients just ended up playing child's games to waste my time.

I also found it unfair of the court to force me to come to court, wasted my time, and never collected anything from me. The court had all of the advantages to close the case, made final decision; instead of having me coming more than five times in court while lawyers kept changing five times every time I came to court. The court should have save me from the pain and suffering when the court, law firm, and their clients knew that I was going to get evicted anyway. The Haitian lady I met in court in 2014 that the landlord intended to rob of more than ten thousand dollars told me that more than two lawyers represented the landlord for the court case she had been. I hope the best came out of her court case since the landlord placed her on the black list not to get any apartments in the city as bad tenants. I would not be surprised if the management and the landlord done the same thing to me. Despite what happened to me, the court would continue to be held responsible and accountable for what happened to me. I am into the mess because of the court event though the court seems not to take full responsibility of messing up my life as someone who wins court cases. There is one of the huge apartment building that has huge parking lot; I went there to get an application. The apartment building is well known because I use to come to the park to play basketball during my high school year. My uncle lives not far away from it. The apartment building located across the street for Medgar Evers College. One morning I went there to get an application. I could not feel out the application because it is stated on the application that I would not be qualified if I face eviction by landlord. I wonder how many apartment buildings done the same thing throughout the City.

The reasons why lawyers kept changing were because the lawyers and their clients trapped not only bring the others in court on purpose without their knowledge, but also the lease and false charges on purpose. Due to these problems, the law firm and their clients went to the Stipulation of Agreement. The outcome of the court case has some details about that part. I want to say that nothing good come out of the stipulation of agreement because of experience I had with one in another issue in the past. I want to say that I was against the stipulation of agreement because of problems and contradiction it came along with. I had been forced by the Judge to accept it; otherwise I would lose the case if I went on trial. I had no choice but to accept it. The same thing happened to me on the problem I had to deal with prior (end of 2016) because I had been forced to accept a stipulation of agreement in order for me to go back to work.

The stipulation of agreement had been designed by people who do not want to lose a fight, case, or dispute. The stipulation of agreement provided them to create more problems to the victim. Therefore, the stipulation of agreement would never be on the favor of the victim. What one would do if he or she finds himself or herself forces by any court existed around the world, to accept any stipulation of agreement, otherwise he or she would lose the court case. The law firm and their clients effectively knew that the stipulation of agreement was worthless, useless, and meaningless for some reasons. The first reason was that the stipulation of agreement was incomplete on purpose by the second lawyer. I had to force the second lawyer to include the full name of the landlord that had been a problem since the day I moved in the apartment, or room; along with the email address and full address of the buildings that they promised to view and choose one apartment out of. The lawyer got the guts and nerve to use me as his slave and told me that I should get that information from the landlord myself. That was not the first time lawyers used me as their slaves to do their jobs for them. It seemed to be that the law firm was helping the landlord to hide his identity. Therefore, the stipulation of agreement was still remained incomplete on purpose despite the struggle to have it complete. I checked the court file after I received the second marshal notice of eviction late again while I was doing an appeal that the court and I knew that it was not going to work. I found out that the name of the landlord had been spelled differently. The first or last name on one of the record spelled as "Freedo" as an example. The name spelled as "Freed" on the stipulation of agreement as an example. I had no idea which one is right or wrong. Therefore, that was not a mistake. That was another "déjà vu" that I witnessed and experienced again. That happened on the small claim that I filed against the chief of the Co-Op in 2013, which the law firm and their clients held responsible and accountable to use fake name without my knowledge. They tried to contradict what I reported in court while doing the process, but put themselves more in trouble. They also affected the court with their mess.

The second reason was that the lawyer changed what he promised to do in front of the Judge verbally before lunch time. The Judge told the lawyer in front of the landlord that to find me an apartment, not a room. The Judge asked them to discuss this out of the courtroom on lunch break.

The lawyer and the landlord did otherwise. The lawyer told me that get out of the apartment, do not pay for the next month rent. Before the Judge said what he had to say before lunch break, I did the best I could to have my response collected along with the report that I updated, on the second attempt. The Judge rejected them with this weird look on his face. I told Judge that I was in the mess because the court. The Judge responded that I was in the mess because I got myself into it. It seemed to be that the court blamed me because it was under my free will I was into this mess instead of desperation and failure of protection from the court case in 2014 which led to illegal eviction by the same court. It was the neglect and abandonment done by the court which led to my desperation. I told the Judge that I had the report and the court had to choose one out of the choices I had. The Judge told me that I got to choose. I told the Judge that I did an appeal about few years ago. The Judge responded by saying that the appeal is not going to work, otherwise checked the appellate office. I told the Judge that I live in a Co-Op, and there was no reply from the Judge about that. It seemed to be that my situation has gotten worse. It seemed to be that I move from limbo to condemnation.

I did check the appellate office many times before, about twice per year (2015-2016). The last time I checked the appellate office was few days after the snow storm in March 2017. The people who worked there told me about the same thing that they did not see any record of my court case and anything about the appeal. The reason I went there was that I called the person who handled the appeal on the day of the snow storm (private company). The person replied by saying that she had done with everything, that was not her responsibility anymore because she sent everything where should have sent them, without provided me information where she sent them. The person added that she does not do this kind of thing anymore. The appellate office told me to check the third floor about the court record and the appeal. The appellate office sent me on the third floor every time I came to them to check on the appeal. I saw the same lady every time I came to the third floor, and told me the same thing about getting in contact with the person I chose on the list to do appeal. The lady even added that the person I chose on the list lied about not doing the same thing anymore when she is still on the list; when I told her what the lady said to me over the phone. It seemed to be that the Judge found out that the appeal was nothing but useless even though the Judge who held the case told me to do it after they went against his decision in 2014. I did the same thing one more time and found the same outcome of it. However, I did something different later on. I went to another floor to get access to the court case. I did get the summery for the previous court case and got the summary for the current case after the eviction took place illegally. I sent both of them along with everything else to Authority. I found out that the appeal was on pending and wonder for how long it would be on pending. I found out that it stated possession denied on the current case and wonder why. There was something I found strange on the current court summary. There was nothing as Sub-landlord included on it for the first roommate whom the landlord and management dropped the entire problem on. That also proved that the law firm and their clients made things up and never reported them to court. I did something when I filled out the form that the second floor gave me. The last papers that the second floor gave me to fill out before or after the eviction took place in 2018 was to accuse the court of evicted me unfairly, wrongfully, and unjustly under identity theft, perjury, and falsify information and documents in 2014, and I want to go back. The Judge should ask me to elaborate of all the accusation I had against the court. The court should have known that I place myself into a position that could have hunt me, or backfire if I did not have any evidence to prove my case, instead of going and draw conclusion to what I said without elaboration. Otherwise, the court found what I said as problem, embarrassment, humiliation, and intimidation because I was the only one who got the guts and nerve to stand up for myself to deal with the court's mess. The people who were in court that day saw and heard everything I said. The court tried to prevent me from creating transition of the previous court case to current court case without having any irrelevance. Otherwise, the court has to prove to me how I got myself into the mess that I had been.

The third reason was the worse than the first two reasons. I came to court after I received the first marshal noticed of eviction. I went to court on the next day, as soon as I received the first marshal notice nearly a week late from the date it has sent to me. I spoke to the lady who worked for the court and collected the email and the text record from me, and stepped out with them. The lady gave them back to me since I told her that I did not come with the rest of the email. She told me to bring them next time. She told me to server the law firm and marshal. I found serving the marshal was kind of new thing to me. I had a court date. I found out that a third lawyer was changed for the court case and tried to bring me backward from everything. I found out from the third lawyer that the law firm does not do stipulation of agreement behind closed door while the lady who worked for the court told the third lawyer about the stipulation of agreement. The third lawyer called the law firm to report about the stipulation of agreement. Therefore, I have been wasted my time into some nonsense and stupidity. The second lawyer had to come in to face the Judge. I found it absurd of the Judge to accuse me of accepting something I tried to avoid, and forced by the Judge to accept it. I have been blamed as a victim there. I wonder if the Judge remembered it was him who told me to accept the stipulation of agreement. Otherwise, the Judge must have eaten from the forgotten food. Therefore, I did not say anything at all on that.

The fourth reason was also the worse than the first two reasons. The stipulation of agreement was not only the waste of time, but also the landlord and management went against it. They both were in the violation of the stipulation of agreement. They both tried to make me do other than what was in the stipulation of agreement. They both tried to send to two places that were not included in the stipulation of agreement. They both tried to have me rent room and continue to be roommates, when the Judge asked them to find me an apartment. They claimed that I could not afford to pay for an apartment because of my income. The wanted me to go on background check when the judge told them not to do so. As I mentioned on the previous book about that some people do not pay anything for their apartments for decades and they happened to be in charge. The previous case I had to deal with was like that. I will not be surprise that the people who gave me hard time on having apartment, do not pay for their apartments or houses for decades. That is what I began to find out that hypocrisy is one of the major problems and sins within human being, the world, and society. Anybody in the country and in the world could not afford to pay for anything regardless how rich they are. Some people are stealing from others to satisfy their needs and claim it is all about survivor of the fittest (survival of the fittest my foot). The housing situation is one of them. The people in charge of the buildings would never take their own money to hire lawyers and spend on luxuries. The previous housing cases

I had to deal with were like that. I wonder how many people in charge of buildings; use the buildings finances to commit other wrongdoings such as funding wars, civil wars, and uprising in other countries for economic gains under the names of the citizens of the country. Therefore, the tenants would be held responsible and accountable for the mess unfairly. Some of the tenants continue to pay more on rent and do not have enough cash for other needs. What about others who face the same problem; but do not have enough money to send back home to help some of their family members back home who depend on them for survival?

The record of the text and email served as proof against the law firm and their clients. The landlord and management knew that one of the addresses that they stated on the stipulation of agreement was not existed anymore due to demolition and construction. The record of the texting and email included after that part. I just found out that one of the addresses was not existed by miracle. The landlord and management wanted me to go to one of the address which located at the corner of the other street, behind the building that had been demolished. I stopped to the building few times while I was in court. There was a problem with the building. It seemed to be that there was no body lived in it. It would be dangerous to live in a building while demolition and construction of a new building happens almost all around it instead next to it. The problem was not only the noises, but also cracks may have occurred to the existence building while digging and drilling deeper underground to build the new building. I know about this because of experience and witness that problem occurred to a place I knew already. I wonder if the existence building could support or withstand all the vibration from the drilling that may happen which may cause either some minor or major cracks throughout the building.

I called the phone number I found online about the other building. I was not going to call because the information about the owner of the building was not available for the public view, which effectively leads to anonymous. I called the number and someone picked up the phone. I spoke with the lady and she told me that she was not affiliated with the landlord and management I mentioned to her about. I began to see that the law firm and their clients tried to make me go against the stipulation of agreement and tried to use anything against me to say that it was all my fault, they tried to help me. Therefore, I would be used as a scapegoat (or patsy) on the problems they created. I had no interest to send anything to the law firm about what had been going on out of the court room for two reasons. The first reason was that the tenant in the building was right when he said that he did not send his response to opponent's lawyer because he does not want them to know what he has in his response. The second reason was that it was a waist of my time and money to do so because the law firm would deny that I sent response to them just to save themselves from the problems that their clients created. The previous cases I had to deal with were evidence of that (second HP action case 2013 and the trial of the Stipulation of Agreement 2014). The same lawyer for both previous cases denied everything I sent to the law firm(s). The reason that happened, which I mentioned in the previous book was that the lawyers are protect their names and their ridiculous reputations. The lawyers used their law firms as corporation so that they would never got blame for the problems they created. They send documents to clients without their names included on envelops. The government and court seem to never take affirmative action on that issue; otherwise they allow it to happen.

However, the law firm and their clients did accuse me by saying that they tried to help me, but I ended up playing games. The record of the texting and email would prove otherwise. No wonder why I did not send my response to the law firm because I want to see how the law firm was about to handle the case. There was something strange that happened on the day I was in court before I accepted and received the useless, worthless, ridiculous, and meaningless stipulation of agreement. It seemed to be that the court allowed the law firm to split the case into two separate court cases with two different index numbers. That was what the gentleman who represented the Judge told me. That could have doubled my pain if I did so for two reasons. The first reason was that I could have being in court more than twice per month for no reason at all. The second reason was that there could be conflicts on dates to be in court for both cases in term of time and dates to be in two different courtrooms at once, or at the same time. I wonder how I could be in two different courtrooms at the same time. The reason why the law firm tried to split court case was that the second lawyer tried to get himself out the mess he created. The outcome would be nothing but repetition of the problems such as served on the wrong zip codes on purpose and everything else. Otherwise, the second lawyer tried to split the case so that the second case should go to a different Judge and courtroom, when the Judge may not have the knowledge the true reason why the court case split, as well as has no knowledge of what happened previously which contribute to the splitting of the court case. Since the law firm knew that I was going to evict illegally, that could be an opportunity for them to send anything without my knowledge to have the court ruled over me unfairly. Therefore, I would be held responsible and accountable for something that the court should have had prevented to begin with. I do not know anything about splitting a court case into two different court cases. The court should have known that I am not a lawyer, and that issue was all on the court to deal with personally without my involvement. I wonder how things going to be if I was forced by the Judge or court to do so, just like the stipulation of agreement.

No wonder I kept the court case together instead of splitting it into two different court cases with different case index number. I also wonder what kind of court case the second case would be. It seemed to be that it would be a small claim. I had been in a small claim before end of 2013 until closer to the mid of 2014. I do not want to be in any small claim case again because of another "déjà vu" that I may experience again. The small claim is the slower case because I have to be in court every four or five months. The previous book had the details about the small claim case. I was under suspicious that the law firm and their clients were up to something about splitting the court case into two different court cases. I found it unfair and ridiculous of the court not to get involve to put a stop by rejecting it. Otherwise, I would be in trouble if let that happen and the court would not take full responsibility and held accountable for allowing the law firm and their clients to do that. I found out that even the court did not get involve immediately when the second lawyer tried to use me as his personal slave to do the job that he was paid to do.

The third reason of the splitting of the case was that the lawyers and their clients trying to get themselves out of the mess that they created. They tried to get themselves out of the lease, fake charges, and brought people in court without their knowledge. The law firm and their clients tried come up with something new and wonder what it would be. I warned the law firm and their clients that they could not do two things at the same time in a court case because that was what happened on the previous case (holdover proceeding 2014). The law firm and their client stated in the stipulation of agreement that they would let go off the fake charges or illegal fees if I complied to leave the apartment on certain date to move in a new apartment. However, the certain date was way past due and their clients never fulfill their promise. Therefore, the law firm and their clients trapped with the lease, wrongful charges on purpose, empty promise on purpose, and useless stipulation of agreement on purpose. The law firm should take more responsibility, as well as held more accountable of the problems than their clients created because the law firm knew about everything but remain in pretense not to know. That was why they kept changing lawyers as excuse and trying to avoid the problems.

The lawyers would be in denial of everything, as well as absurd of them if they say they did not know how many times lawyers had been changed; brought me backward into the court case while I moved forward with the court case. No wonder I stated on the previous book about that there is nothing sweeter than trapping a lawyer with his/her client, particularly when both of them play nasty and dirty games to destroy the life of innocent and vulnerable people. There is one more thing I need to say which concerns about witness. Witness happened to be an issue there. The landlord and the second lawyer stated behind closed door about having witness on August 2018. Therefore, they did not have any witnesses. That is also another "déjà vu" I had to deal with there on witness. That happened on the trial of the holdover proceeding in 2014, and it repeated on the current case.

Stipuplation of agreement Or Settlement

1) *Proceeding settled as follows: final judgment of possession entered in favor of petioner Iss and of the warrant for with execution stayed through 8/31/18 for respondent to vacate.*
2) *Petitioner agrees to two units available for viewing rental w/in 7 days which are available for move in 8/31 or earlier if the respondent agrees after inspection to take one of the units be shall be approved without application process. Address ### & ### prospect place*

3) *Conditional on timely vacatur petitioner waives all rental arrears through August 2018.*
4) *Full and timely vacatur involves leaving apartment in broom swpt condition free at all accupants and possessions items left behind shall be deemed abandoned. Keys to be surrendered to management.*
5) *Respondent agrees to contact A** F***** at (###)###-#### for viewings.*
6) *Proceeding discontinued against all other named respondents as petitioner confirms they have vacated.*
7) *Upon default petioner may execute on warrant by service at marshal's notice.*
8) *Respondent agrees to allow petitioner to show apartment upon 24 hour notice.*

The fifth Issue

The court wrongdoing

That was not my problem if the court did not collect the response I sent to the law firm and their clients by email and mail, including the report I had for the court case. I was under suspicious that the court and law firm wanted the landlord to get away with the problem. I would get blame by the court if I came to court empty handed. I was fully prepared to deal with the court case. I found it lame and absurd of the law firm and their clients brought me in court meanwhile they kept the court file empty. The law firm never reported to the court about that I sent response to them over the wrongful charges that happened on purpose. I did not see how the court would take care and solve the court case effectively if the court did not collect my response, but allowed the law firm and their clients play nasty and dirty games. I also do not think that the people who worked for the court would do an effective job at reporting about what actually happened or took place behind closed doors. I did not know what was going to happen to me if I come empty handed after I received the first marshal notice of eviction, which was almost a week late from the date the notice sent out for delivery. I came with all of the texting record and most of the email record to review by the court in order for the court to see what actually took place outside the court. The girl I mentioned early about the court evicted people without court dates and trial also told me that the court did not care about collecting your response and it was such a waste of time to have them.

Therefore, it was unfair of the court to ignore most of what I have at my disposal. It took me time, energy, dedication, and sacrifice to write response and report for the court to collect. It was disrespectful of the court to ignore them. I would continue to do my part in order to protect myself from the system. I would rather being prepared instead of not being prepared at all. I would put myself in a deeper hole if I am not prepared. The reason why I want the court to collect my response was that to move the court case forward and faster so that I want to minimize on the population of people that come to court every day. I mentioned in the previous book that the population of people who came to court seems to never minimize. It seems to be that each and every individual in the population has to make more than four trips in court for their court cases. I did the best I could to have the court case to be over on two trips. It was the court that allowed me to waste my time when I tried to avoid my time wasted. Those times that had been wasted also affect my job because it was hard to find someone to work my shift for few hours or the whole shift when I took off to be in court for no reason at all.

There was something I witnessed on the second floor while I took care the first marshal notice I received late by mail. A gentleman, African American probably in his 60's or mid 60's, talked out loud said that the President of the country is screwing the court, no wonder nothing never gotten resolved in court. There was another thing I witnessed on the floor same while I was in line, took care the second marshal notice that I also received late by mail. This lady worked for legal aid, walking around, sent out message out loud to apply for apartment. A lady who was in line, African American in her 50's or mid 50's, said out loud to the lady that she applied for apartment at the legal aid office and did not work out. There was no argument or response from the lady who worked for the legal aid, but she simply walked away. Therefore, the housing situation is far more worse than anyone could have had imagined it to be.

There was something else that I witnessed on the first day and the second day of court. I saw two ladies. They were not in the courtroom while I was waiting for the court cased to be called by the court. I saw the first lady (African American probably in her 30's), when the first lawyer called me out of the courtroom and I walked away. The second lady (may be Latina probably in her 30's as well) showed up out of the blue after I got the next court date, to have the landlord showed up in court in August 2018. I saw the lady and the second lawyer gave each other smiles while I walked away. I wonder what was behind that smile. I always wonder when people smile and laugh like that, if they can get away with problem, financial crime, prejudice, discrimination, injustice despite the facts that the court decision ruled over or against them. I find smile and laugh like this weird, strange, shocking, and disturbing. The previous cases I had to deal with (HP action cases, small claim case, and Holdover Proceeding case) full with this type of behaviors. Therefore, this is another "déjà vu" that I experienced all over again.

The court would also be held responsible and accountable for the paper that the law firm gave to me after the eviction took place. The law firm stated that they accepted the stipulation of settlement. I do not know if I was settling for money. There was nothing stated that in the stipulation of agreement that I would receive reward for the court case. Otherwise, the law firm tried to turn the stipulation of agreement into stipulation of settlement because one part of it had the word settlement. One reason that the law firm tried to turn the stipulation of agreement into settlement was that because there was not anywhere on the paper stated that it was a stipulation of agreement or stipulation of settlement. The second lawyer came to court with it and stated verbally that he had something in writing; while he did not include that in writing that it was a stipulation of agreement. Therefore, the lawyer tried to be clever. There was nothing on the paper sound like it was a stipulation of settlement. I also do not know if there is such thing as stipulation of settlement. I wonder how one looks like if there is one existed. The court summary stated only stipulation, and wonder stipulation of what.

The law firm tried to be clever with the case they had against me because they thought that I do not have record of what happened since day one. I did not began to keep my personal record about what happened on the third or fourth trip in court when I found that the court is not doing anything at all to close the case. The law firm took risk to that. The law firm thought that I was unable to remember what happened few weeks or few months ago and used that as opportunity to make case against me when they knew what actually took place in the past. It would be wrong for the court to tell me to send response to the law firm when it was already late to do so. I would not hesitate to drag the court into that because the court witnessed all of what the law firm had against me as cases.

The Sixth Issue

Audio and written Transcript

I wonder if everything that had been said in court, behind closed doors, and brought to the Judge attention are available on audio and written transcript without missing anything. No wonder I keep my personal record in case if the court is not keeping the records of everything that had been going on. The same thing applies to the court file. I looked inside the court file while wasting my time to file for appeal that I know would denied at the appellate office. I did not see any record of what happened throughout the court times and dates, on the court file. I read few of the court documents and I could not make sense out of them. The words and term the court use on the documents was knew to me. It might take me time to read and analyze them to make sense out of them. However, I did not have the time. The court documents on the court file was a lot. I also wonder if the court tried to cover up all of the offenses and wrongdoings that the law firm and their clients committed towards and against me, and the court offense and wrongdoing towards me and against me as well. I mentioned about those offenses and wrongdoings already. I also wonder if the court collected the ridiculous cases the law firm had against me after I was evicted illegally. I received the law firm cases late in court by the fifth lawyer, which considered as foul, unfair, and problems which will explain on the last issue.

Some of the few reasons why there could have been missing audios and written transcripts was the court do not want their wrongdoings on record. The Judge should have been careful when I challenged the court, by accusing the court that I was into the mess because of the court. The Judge's reaction was wrong to blame me for no reason without elaboration.

The other thing that the Judge said concerning about the appeal was troubling. I wonder how the other side would handle the case when they have to hear all of the wrongdoings done not only by the law firm and their clients, but the court contributed to the wrongdoings to some degree. Therefore that could be a big embarrassment for the court to behave the way it was toward me and the case. I remembered I met with the gentleman when I left court probably on September 2019, on his way out. He was an African American around his 30's or mid 30's. He was mad at the court the way the people who work at the court are. He said he has his bachelor degree and found that the people in court do not have respect for him, but treated him as dirt. He had to deal not only with housing situation, but also personal situation that lead to have his license revoked seems to be over his girlfriend issue. He had problem with his roommate over his girlfriend which may have led to his license revoked. Things got physical there. I could not say or mention in the book what cause the problem without his consent. I just simply leave thing the way it is. He aware the problem of paying more money for a small room and feels uncomfortable of sharing toilet with strangers.

The Seventh Issue

Evicted illegally on purpose without protection again

Despite all that I had been through in court all of the court cases, the law firms and their clients went against the Judge's decision to evict me. That is another "Deja vu" that I am experienced again. That was what happened after the Trial of the Holdover Proceeding case 2014. On the current case the Judge made his decision by using the word *"let me vacate with dignity"* which included almost at the end of the Judge's decision. The word "vacate" had been used in the previous court case (Holdover Proceeding) in 2014. The Judge's second decision in 2014 stated that *"there are no ground to vacate the judgement enter after the trial of the holdover proceeding. Respondent motion is denied. The marshal notice may be executed. Any necessary re-service must be made by mail."* That also prove that the court evicted me without any protection in 2014. The word "vacate" has two legal meanings. The first meaning is to cancel. The second meaning is to leave. The law firms and their clients know that they never have cases against me. They both take their power, privileges, right, liberty, freedom, and democracy into their hands to force me out of the apartment without proving any cases against me. The case that the law firm gave me in court after I was evicted full with problems. Yet, the law firm did not include all of the wrongdoings that the lawyer(s) and their clients committed towards and against me, besides the perjury. Speaking of perjury, I do not think that the law firm stated what type of perjury they committed. The type of perjury the law firm committed run at their deepest level. The law firm was intentionally to do wrongdoing towards and against me under prejudice and injustice. All of the seven issues are not the only case I have against the law firm and their clients, but all the wrongdoings I mentioned or indicated earlier before of getting to the seven issue parts, such as corruption, extortion, robbery, slavery, prejudice, discrimination, disrespectful, false accusation, wrongfully accused on purpose, wrongful label on purpose, serve on the wrong zip code on purpose, and injustice.

The perjury itself is an issue. The law firm stated vaguely about perjury without any specification of the type of perjury they had committed. I wonder if the law firm tried to say that they do not know what their clients were up to, or pretend not to know what their clients were up to. Therefore, the law firm and their clients knew what they had been doing, and doing so on purpose. It is absurd of the law firm to omit, or exclude all of the major offenses out of the court case that they had against me, and committed towards me, besides the perjury that the law firm committed throughout the court case. The same thing applied to the court as well about omitting, or excluding all major offenses that the law firm had done against me and towards me. Despite all that had been happened, the law firm ended up playing the innocent game out of the court case. The law firm and their clients evicted me by force and the rest of my belongings may have been stolen. The law firm and their clients were not only forced themselves in the apartment, but also forced themselves in the room I was in, that was locked. I had very few of my belonging remained in the room. I have very few of my belongings in the two bathrooms, small kitchen cabinets or draws. I had few documents that were in few plastic bags. There was about seven hundred dollars of my personal property had been missing. There are more details of what I lost at the end of the outcome of the court case. I send everything to the authority as well. I also sent the summaries of 2014 and 2018 court case to authority and hoping they do something about them. Otherwise, I would take matters into my own hand. I am still taking matters into my own hand no matter what because these types of people need to be exposed of their wrongdoings.

I did not have time to get the remaining of my belongings out of the apartment because I had to be out of town that Saturday night. I did two trips to the storage from morning to the afternoon by bus and train while the public transportation is slowed on the weekends. Each trip lasted about three hours, including the walk and made place in the storage for the remaining belongings. Everything was already out of the apartment when I receive the first marshal notice. I have waited until the time expired and nothing happened. I brought everything back nearly a week and half later which was a waste of my time because I received another marshal notice about few days later. I decided to get most of them out again as soon as I left court. I took most of the belongings to work and a friend's house temporally. The rest went to the storage again. I could not fit everything in the storage because it was already full, as I mentioned before. I had to make up to five trips just to get my belongings out of the apartment all by myself by using public transportation.

It would be unfair of the court to blame for not doing the appeal for two reasons. The first reason is that I continued not having a physical address to do an appeal when the court knows that it was a problem to begin with. It was wrong, unfair, and absurd of the court to ask me to do the appeal when I did not have a physical address to do it five years ago. I used someone else address to do the appeal without their approval. There are more details about that on the previous book. The second is that the court does not use P.O. Box to do appeal. I include that part on the previous book that was based on suspicious. Therefore, my suspicious was right. I just found out about that when I got access to the courts summaries. The third floor told me that I was unable to change any address from the court case five years ago to a new address and the court did not use P.O. Box to do appeal. I had been told that they will send documents to that address even though I was currently not there anymore. The court never mentioned anything about doing an appeal for the current court case, when the court would not be happy about the answer I would give them on the matter of the appeal.

There were two legal aids offices that I went to find out if people could help me with my problem. However, I mentioned on the previous book that I went to one of the legal aids that the court told me to choose and go to get help, which turned out to be a big waste of my time. The court seemed to run by bunch of people which make me wonder if they know what they are doing, or just done things on purpose to make people waste their times. I will never have faith and hope that any legal aid would solve my housing cases in the future, particularly the experience I had with legal aid in the past. The first legal aid that I went to was located a block away from the housing court. I did not know about it until I explained my situation to someone who came to relieve at work one Sunday afternoon in June 2018. She gave me the address of the legal aid and told me that the legal aid helped her with her housing situation. She told me that her case did not take more than two trips in court. She added that the legal aid came in and told the landlord's lawyer that the landlord did not have cases against her, close the case, and made the landlord paid about ten thousand dollars to her. I could not draw conclusion at what had been said to me. I met with the same employee a year later from another place. She asked me about how the housing situation had been for me. She was surprised that I told her about what had been happening and told me that the system would never change. She even told me that she was homeless and went to live in a hotel with her child. She added that her lawyer told her that why she did not give the money to the landlord instead. That was something I would not take from my lawyer or anybody. It seemed to be that her lawyer was at the landlord's side instead of hers. I am under suspicious that the housing court and the city want the landlords to stay around and being under pretentious of doing something about the housing issues and problems.

I went to the legal aid for the first time, few days after I received the stipulation of agreement in August 2018, after work. The people who worked there told me that it was late to take me in and they have a small office in the housing court. I went to the housing court right away and I spoke to one of the gentleman that was in the office. He looked at the stipulation of agreement and told me that I did fine and the landlord could not get himself out of the stipulation of agreement. Otherwise, the landlord would be in trouble with the Judge. The gentleman knew the Judge and told me that the Judge was a tough Judge. The gentleman told me that came back to the office for help if anything went wrong. I did that and I did not receive any help from them when I came to them after court day on September 2018. I spoke with somebody else. The second person, a lady, gave a different meaning of the stipulation of agreement. The lady told me something that the Judge said on August that the landlord was a good landlord because the landlord tried to find me a place to live. She added just like the Judge said that no landlord would ever do that, the same way. That was not true, the law firm and the landlord stole that from the response I sent to them, which never collected in court, but rejected by the court twice. I told them to find me another place if they want me to leave the apartment. The lady even said that it is right and lawful to serve anyone without their knowledge if they are not in their apartments when I spoke to her about that. I could not draw any conclusion by what said to, but remained objective out of them.

I went back to the legal aid office when the court denied my appeal and gave me paper that had the list of legal aids office to choose from to go to. I had another "Déjà vu" there. That was what happened when the shitty, useless, and worthless appeal that the lawyer gave me and stole my seventeen hundred dollars in 2014, which it was refused by the Appellate office. However, the list was shrinking because there were about less legal aid office included on the list than there were in 2014. I went back to the place. I sat there and they confiscated some of the court documents and told me fill out form. Few minutes later, I have been told to stop and do not continue filling out the form. They told me that they could not help because I made more than twenty four thousand dollars a year. They added that I could afford to get a lawyer. I found so strange that I pay taxes every year on a service that would eventually unable to help me due to my income.

I checked the second one because someone who knew about what I had been through in the last past five years, told me to check that legal aid. That person gave me advice on the previous book and knew about the current book. The second place was less likely to be legal aid because it sets up separately from the others and it was not included on the list that the court gave me. I called them and made an appointment with them about a week after thanksgiving's holyday in 2018. I witnessed an issue from a family that came in few minutes after me. The daughter and the mother explained their issue to one of the lady who worked in the place, concerning about the landlord of their apartments' building. I heard them said that the landlord did not want the mother to stay in the apartment anymore after the death of her husband that happened recently, and the wife could not inherited the husband's apartment even after her husband's death. I wondered if that was included on the proprietary lease. Even though if it does, I said before that proprietary lease had been design to be in favor of the landlord, just like the law and institution on slavery was in the favor of the slave masters to do whatever they want to do as fair, just, virtue, and right. The lady who worked at the place could only said in a passive tone of voice 'really, how could this happened', and did not say anything else at all. I heard everything and I told them that the problem is a universal on the housing issue. The lady who worked asked me if I was in the same situation. I replied said even though my father is still around, the board did the same thing to my mother about that she could not inherited my father. I wondered how a case like this would handle if the family went to court. That problem is not new; it has been going on since the day mankind gave birth to economics. Everything that happened now resulted from the past, particularly nearly one thousand years ago and continued to get worst.

The lady might have problem to apply for Medicare because she needed a physical address to apply for Medicare. That is the problem that my mother keeps dealing with since the eviction took place in September 2014. She is still unable to apply for Medicare due to physical address issue. I mentioned on the previous book that it is not everything that one could do on P.O. Box. The government and the others in charge never do anything about this common problem in the city. I did the best I could to do that but the system could care less about the eviction that my mother faces. I got forced into the problem by family when I told them I did it before and it did not work. I could not even use my relative address to do that if they live under landlord. I mentioned before that the landlords are part of the system because there are certain documents that the landlords need to approve and sign for the tenants in order for them to apply and receive Medicare. The light and gas bills are part of them. The letter that the place would give you to fill must fill by the landlords for approval. I wonder how the situation would turn out for tenants if the landlords do not want to fill and sign form for the tenants. Would that be done on carelessness or anonymous? Any landlords would never want their names to be out there when they are in illegal business that take place in their buildings. Who knows how many people suffer like that from their landlords due to Medicare issue. Therefore the court and government should be blamed for that because they give the landlords right, power, and privilege on the private lives of the tenants. I could not use my uncle's address to do that for my mother. My uncle knows it would be impossible not only for that matter, but also the issue he had with the landlord over his apartment remains without maintenance, and being in court with the landlord many times. Therefore, the landlord would use anything as an advantage and excuse to have cases against my uncle, to accuse my uncle is under violation of his lease without the landlord's approval. I have been in court already and people like to make ridiculous cases against me, yet changes things when they got caught just to avoid or escape offences. The previous book has a lot of details about them.

I sat in the place for nearly an hour, and my name called out to see someone. I spoke to the lady behind closed door. The lady was about close to her thirties, African-American, may have been Haitian- American. There was an African-American male probably in his mid-fifty's was there as well collecting documents from me (may be mix with Hispanic descent). I already put on the application that I was looking an apartment. I gave the lady the court documents and the summaries of both court cases. The gentleman took them from me and made copies of them. I told the lady that I already made my decision to send everything to Authority on December 31, 2018 because I am getting sick and tired the way the court operated. She told me that she did not blame me, and I must do so. I spoke to her about the book that I publish on the previous housing court issue. She told me that lawyer never got punish for their wrongdoings because they good at cover up their mess. She was right about that because the system would never punish lawyers even though there are strong evidences to prove of their wrongdoings. Some lawyers behave like bad police and got away if their wrongdoings because the court and the city allowed them to get away with wrongdoings. Therefore, lawyers like that protected by the system, just like bad police do. It was evident on the current case that the lawyers committed wrongdoings towards me and knowing that they would never get severe punishment for their wrongdoings. The Lady also added that landlord may not want me to be back in the apartment, but pay me to be out of the apartment. I wonder how much the landlord would offer me as a color person. It is also evident that the law firm and their clients made me waste my time, and the court also contributed to that, when they know that they would evict me anyway.

The current and previous cases I had to deal with was that the lawyers continue to come to court, committed wrongdoings. My countryman I mentioned in the previous book who worked at the real estate company was right. He told me that landlords do otherwise, despite the court order and decision prevent them to do so. The lawyers are the one that contributed to that as well. However, it depend what lawyers who may have punish severely for their wrongdoings, due to racial matters. Let's go back to the last thing that the people at the place told me before I left. The gentleman told me that the place he worked had been excluded from everything that happened in any court cases when the court cases went to higher places. The same thing applied to both of my court cases, particularly the previous court case. The gentleman added that he did not know what is going to happen with both court cases when the other side makes the last decision on the court cases. Therefore, all they told me that they would the best they could, and they will let me know about everything in few weeks by mail. However, I have not heard from them ever since and I had no intention of calling them or go back to them. I was just hope to get a response, even though I already knew to some degree that they would unable to do anything out of the current and previous court cases. I gave them the P.O. Box address to change the address that I gave the first legal aid I went on the day I was evicted five years ago and used the address to do the appeal. The place found that information while they were doing the process for me.

However, I did go back to the same place a week before thanksgiving holiday again and hope for the best, which did not happened. I met with the same gentleman. I told him and the lady who set up the appointment that I came a year ago and I did not receive any response from them. They tried to blame for not calling them when it was their responsibilities to send me response or call. That is weird of any places to blame the victims of what is their responsibilities. I had been told to fill out the same I did last year and told me I must do so every time I come to the place. I had been told that the forms are like intake. The gentleman told me that lawyer usually come every Wednesday to the place just to get cases from clients. The gentleman told me that the place is affiliated to the legal aid located on Court Street. It seemed to be that I went back to the same people who did not do anything for me when I was evicted. They could not help me because the case five years ago was complexed for them to deal with because that was not what they do. The previous book has a lot of details about that. They were the one who told me to go to one of the floor to start the process of the appeal. That is why I keep blaming the court for sending me to places that would not do anything for my cases. The appellate office is the contributor on that problem when they denied appeals and sent me to any of the places that they have on list for nothing at all. I spoke with the lawyer, Caucasian in his fifties, who was there that day. It was a waste of my time because the lawyer did not take the summaries of the court cases from me to make copies of. The lawyer told that it was too late to do something about both cases. The lawyer asked me to give the address where live now. I told the lawyer that I could not disclose that information because I was already living there illegally, and being homeless ever since. I told the lawyer that I only used my P.O. Box to get mail. The lawyer even asked me how much I got to my bank account. That was what the gentleman asked five years ago. I asked the lawyer why he asked that, and it purposed. The lawyer told me that he wanted to find out if I qualify to get help from them. The lawyer told me I should not have about fifty thousand dollars or over in my bank account. Otherwise, I would not qualify, but hired private lawyer. The lawyer even told me that there is nothing he could not do to the first court case due to the lack of resources. That was almost the same thing that the gentleman told me last year and again before I began spoking with the lawyer. There was something that the gentleman told me before I saw the lawyer. The gentleman told that the Government even goes above the Supreme to do things. The gentleman also added that the country continues to run under one hundred years of expiration dates. The gentleman also added who would come to change things. I responded by saying that if he is willing to take a bullet for it, just like president Kennedy (many more after him). The gentleman shook his head up and down after I said that. There is a current issue that happened with the new NYPD police commissioner. The new police commissioner had been force to resign because of firing the police officer who use an illegal choke hold and kill the African American who said he was unable to breathe from it. Other police officers who could have done the same thing would get fire automatically regardless of how many years they have been on the police force base on their racial background. The police commissioner is very brave to take some action like that when others before him may have been scared or careless to do anything about that some police officers are shooting innocent African Americans which may appear as murder, instead of otherwise.

There is one thing I need to add about the court. Some people I used to talk to about the court system said that the lawyers and the Judges are into it together. I want to say whether it is true or not, that is their business. I did my part and if the court and the lawyers try to do that in my court case, the court would be held responsible and accountable to let the lawyers and their clients walk away from the problems they created. There are laws that prevent lawyers and Judges to get involve into funny businesses. This book and the previous prove that all of the battles that I have been were to fight them in the middle or the center. Fighting the fight in the middle or center is not an easy fight because that is where everything comes to you at once, just like lines of symmetry. Therefore one has to be very strong, very skillful, very able, and very capable to handle everything that comes towards you. However, based on what I see so far on the previous case and current case is that the law firm and their clients seem to be the one control the housing court. They continue to be disrespectful toward the court, by going against the Judges' decisions to evict tenants.

The outcome of Non-Payment (Case Index # Omitted)

It was on 4/18 I went to the shelter located on the east of Manhattan to see if anyone could helped me. I did so because I was threaten by the landlord and management that the other roommates and I must leave the apartment at (#### Pacific st Bk NY #####) on 5/31/18, due to unfair charges that they imposed on us. The lady I spoke with, after spending four hours or more at the shelter, told me that she would put me on the system in case if the eviction actually took place. However, I spent two nights at the shelter as the date approached for us to give up the apartment (5/30/18 & 5/31/18). I did so because I did not want to come to work on night and found out that the landlord and management changed the lock on me, even though I paid the rent. The shelter did not help me to apply for apartment. The lady I spoke with that night told me that I do not have enough income because it is cost $ 1,500 to live in one bedroom apartment. I reply to her that even though there were mice and roaches in the apartment. She had some personal problem to deal with and wonder why they hire someone likes that to work in a shelter. She told me to meet with someone on the afternoon for that. I met with someone and she told me to call her in case if the eviction took place. She found places that rented room on price range $800 and up. I spent two nights in the shelter and the place is filthy and smelly. On May 25, 2018, before I spent the two nights at the shelter, I went to court to have a court date after we had been served by the landlord and management. I had been told by the clerk that my court date is in a week from the day I filed for court date. The clerk told me that she was unable to collect my response from me due to the fact that it was not notarized. I did not know anything about notarized my response. I did not do that at the Supreme Court case (2014), as well as at the Holdover Proceeding case before that (2014). I also did not know if this is a new thing going in court or not. Otherwise, the Clerk said to bring my response in court by hand.

It was in the morning of **6/1/18** I went to court in the courtroom ###, over the charges that the landlord and management imposed on me and the others. The first lawyer that they hired said in front of the person (male) who represented the Judge said I must paid over $10,000 dollars fees because I have to be held responsible for the debt of the other roommates. The lawyer also added that I have to be held responsible to pay over $3,000 dollars on monthly rent because I had to pay for the other rooms that were empty as well. The lawyer claimed all of that had been said in the least which I never had and received from the real estate (name omitted) that sent me to the room/apartment in June 2017. I got the room by the real estate (name omitted) individually, not collectively, yet no one told me about any lease until management told me by emails before I went to court. The person who represented the Judge said to the lawyer if he never had been in the apartment to see how things were. The lawyer replied, no. I added by saying that the money I had been told I owed was nothing but added on the lawyer's fees. I also added that if the charges that the landlord and management, along with the lease were lawful and constitutional. They both responded, yes at the same time. The gentleman told the lawyer that to send the bill to his email address. The lawyer called someone to have it sent. The gentleman who worked for the Judge gave me a copy. I let the gentleman knew that I never receive the May 2018 bill. I came to court with the April 2018 bill. I even asked the gentleman to collect my response, but never did. The Judge was in the room looking for something and walked out immediately.

The gentleman decided to set another court date and stated that it would be a trial on **7/13/18** in the morning and the landlord must be attended. I spent about 5 hours in court on 6/1/18. I also spent about 5 hours in court on 7/13/18. After I spent about few hours sat in the same courtroom, a lawyer came and asked for application from the person who held the court files about the court case. The person told the lawyer that he must asked the Judge for that. Therefore, lawyers had been changed for the case. It was a second time that the second lawyer tried to call me out of the courtroom and I rejected by saying what he would said to me is worthless, useless, and meaningless. I said the same thing to the first lawyer as well on 6/1/18. The name of the person appear on court record was (full name of the sub-landlord). Both lawyers told me that I should not be in court. Meanwhile, I was in court I saw the two lawyers I had been dealing with on the previous cases **(HP action cases 2013 & holdover proceeding 2014)** I had before. They pretended that they were looking for their clients in the courtroom. It was not a coincidence that I was in the same courtroom with them, but the law firm knew about them and decided to contact them, after I sent response to the law firm concerning about the charges, and the reasons why I got myself into the mess I was in. They came to the courtroom individually in about one hour away from another, and left the courtroom in few seconds, after they look around to identify me. It seemed to be that the law firm contacted them. When I faced the Judge, the second lawyer said that the landlord could not be in court due to the Jewish holiday. I responded by saying that was preposterous. I told the Judge that he could collect my response from me and did not have to be in court anymore. The Judge replied, no, I must be here. I also let the Judge knew that someone by the name, name omitted, claimed to be the manager, told me I should have left the apartment, last week. The Judge said not to worry about that. Therefore nothing collected from me by the court yet. The judge added that he discussed the case with other Judges. The Judge said someone would give another court date that should be a trial. The Judge asked me to choose the date for the trial. I could not choose a day of the next week, but only a day of the next following week. I also let the Judge knew that the first roommate left end of April 2018, the second roommate left beginning of May 2018, and the third left beginning of June 2018, when the Judge asked me about them. I wondered if it is legal to serve the first two roommates without their knowledge and let the court knew that we had been force out.

I spoke with another person who worked for the Judge, behind close door about the case. I let her and the lawyer knew that I was in the mess because of the court. The lawyer asked me if I had other case going on. I responded, yes. The lawyer asked me about if the apartment is in good condition. I responded that I only spoke about my room, and the other rooms were none of my business. Early morning on **8/1/18**, I spent about fours in courtroom ###, and I finally saw who the landlord was. The Judge asked me to follow the landlord's lawyer, with the court file on his hand to courtroom ###. At about one hour and a half later, the court case had been discussed again behind closed by the person who worked for the Judge in the room. I made another attempt to have my response, the report, and everything else collected and added in the court file. The person said I could not do that now, but waited until I faced the Judge to do so. The only thing that person did was to look at the rent receipts and collected the record of what the real estate (name omitted) sent to me by email for the room, along with the last emails I sent to management, since everything stapled together. I even challenged the landlord lawyer to put things on paper instead of saying them verbally. The person asked the landlord if he collected all of the keys. The landlord reply yes without stated that where his office located. I replied by saying that one key remained in the apartment, unless someone went in the apartment to get the key without my knowledge. Later one I asked the lawyer to put everything that needed to be done on paper when I found the court failed to do so. All the court did was to collect a Lease that I did not know about, or had a copy of. The landlord even stated that he had witnesses and I wondered who because I never met and saw who worked for the landlord and management. I let both Judges (### and ###) knew about the trickery and never knew and seeing the Lease. The real estate (name omitted) never told me about any Lease. I just signed papers and got my room individually. Why should I pay over $10,000 that I did not owed and over $3000 on monthly rent by myself? I should pay for other rooms that are empty. It had been stated in the lease that I did not know anything about. These are some of the big issues and problems throughout the court case. I let both Judges knew that we have been forced out and we had been served late. They also led to Corruption, extortion, robbery, economic gangsters, and mafia. The real estate (name omitted) never told me anything about the lease in May 2017.

When I faced the Judge about 12:30pm, I had to repeat myself about the dates the other roommates moved out and the other two had been served without their knowledge. I made a third attempt to have the court and the Judge to collect my response and the report. The Judge refused by saying that why I gave him this. I let the Judge knew that I was into this mess because of the court. The Judge replied that I got myself into this mess. I let the Judge knew that that I have options on the report and the court must choose one of these options. The Judge replied that I got to choose. I let the Judge knew that I lived in a Co-Op and I did the appeal about 3 years ago. The Judge replied the appeal may not work, otherwise checked the 15th floor. The lawyer replied that he did not know any of that. The Judge added later on that I did the right thing about not leaving the apartment, but the others were in trouble. The Judge was also wondered if I was defending the other roommates on their absence, but focus on myself. The Judge told me that the landlord seemed to be nice since he wanted to move me to another building. That is not true; I was the one who asked management to find me another place. There are more details on the email I sent to management and the law firm. The landlord and his lawyer tried to use what I sent to them as their defense. The Judge also told the landlord and his lawyer that I should not go to background check for the apartment. Since it was closed to lunch time the Judge told me that the lawyer and his client must talked about that and came back at 2pm with decision. As I walked out the courtroom with the landlord and his lawyer, the lawyer said to me that he did not know if it was going to be guaranteed that the landlord will send to another building and did not pay the August 2018 rent and leave the apartment. I replied to the lawyer that we had to come back in front of the Judge. The landlord reaction was to yell "oh, oh", and then I walked away.

At approximately 2:30pm, I faced the person that represent the Judge in the courtroom (not behind close door this time) and I told them that about what the lawyer said to me. He tried to take me out of the courtroom and I refused. The person who represented the Judge said be quiet and not to upset the Judge. The gentleman said that he assumed that what I claimed said to me. I replied by saying that I heard what the lawyer said to me loud and clear. When we faced the Judge in about 10 minutes later, the landlord was not there, the Judge found that the lawyer changed what he said before lunch time. The lawyer also added that I got different meaning by what he said to me. The lawyer stepped out and came back with a **stipulation of agreement.** The lawyer stated verbally that his client had two buildings to check two apartments, and choose one. The lawyer did not include any of the addresses of the buildings in the stipulation of agreement; along with the full name of the landlord. I found that the lawyer got the gust and nerve to tell me to call the landlord to get all of that information from him. The court never stepped in to stop it which considered as a major offense and disrespectful toward me from the lawyer. That also counted as slavery. I replied to the lawyer by saying with a little anger that he got paid to do his job. The lawyer went out with the stipulation of agreement and came back few minutes later. The lawyer did not include the borough, zip codes, and apartment numbers in the stipulation of agreement. The lawyer and his law firm knew that his client had been committed perjury on the zip code they served me to come to court. The lawyer and the landlord served me on purpose on zip code ##### instead of zip code #####. Therefore, that was not a mistake. The person who represented the Judge asked me if I want the stipulation of agreement by itself or included with everything previously. I did not know what the difference is, but replied that to include it with everything previously. The lawyer was there and was laughing. I was forced by the court to accept the stipulation of agreement because the

Judge said I would lose the case if I went on trial. He even asked the person who worked for him to make a schedule for that. I replied it was fine and there was no need for that.

I spent about 30 minutes waiting for the Judge to sign the stipulation of agreement. I did not know if the lawyer or the landlord signed it, since the landlord was not in the courtroom. I got a copy of the stipulation of agreement and the lawyer walked out of the courtroom without gotten the other copy before I left. I called the landlord at the entrance of the courtroom, before I left court. I left court around 4:30pm and spent close 9 hours in court that day. I told the landlord about that he knew what needed to be done over the phone. The landlord replied that his lawyer told him about everything. I had the records of the texting and email of what had been going on throughout August 2018. I sent the copies of both along with everything else that the court did and did not collect from me to authority. I went to one of the Verizon stores one Saturday afternoon and found that they could not give me the texting record even though I represented myself in court. They told me that only the Judge could issue warrant for the texting record, and lawyers included. I had been told the same thing when I called the company on my phone few days later. The landlord even called on August 8, 2018 while I was at work and said that he was trying to help when he knew that he was not. I decided to hang up the phone when the conversation did not get me anywhere.

I made a shocking discovery about one of the buildings was not existed anymore, on August 27, 2018, due to demolition that is due on winter 2019. ### Prospect place was not existed. The address of #### Bedford Avenue had been used to cover up for ### & ### Prospect place. I opened the mail box on the second Sunday of September 2018 and found that the marshal notice was among other mails. I had to call out for work immediately to be in court on the next day. However, I thought I was going to be in court for three to four hours, but I decided to call to have the whole day off. I went on the 2nd floor to fill out paper (same ones that I filled out on the holdover proceeding case 2014). I was sent to courtroom ### in about an hour and half later. I sat in the courtroom for about two hour and a half. I met and spoke with the same lady behind close door. The Judge was not in the courtroom. The lady called the marshal to let the marshal knew that the notice had been received. The lady kept taking note about what

I said to her and collected the texting and email from me, and told me to wait out. I also told her that I did not get any chance to get the record of the last email, and I will have everything with me next time.

The lady went out of the courtroom to another courtroom and came back about 10 minutes later. The lady called out my name and told me come with her behind close door. The lady gave me back the texting and email, and told me to come back with them next time; along with one month rent, since I told her I had the copies of August and September rent. The lady told in the mean time I had to serve the marshal and law firm. She told me I could either do them in person or by mail. I did both by mail because both law firm and marshal located far in Queens. I even told her that I may go to the (authority name omitted). The lady replied that the (authority name omitted) would not do anything. I left court at about 2pm to go to the post office in Church Avenue. The court date was on 9/18/18 at 2pm. I worked 5 hours that day and went to court immediately. On **9/18/18** at 2pm, I came back to room ###, and about 30 minutes later the court case transferred to courtroom ###. The Judge who was in courtroom ### happened to be in courtroom ###. Before I went to courtroom ###, there was a lady approached me, without stated her name and where she came from, about five minutes before the courtroom ### opened at 2pm. She tried to bring me back from the beginning of everything when she did not know anything about the stipulation of agreement. It was a client in the courtroom told me that the lady was a lawyer and came from the law firm that the landlord hired to handle the case; after the lawyer accused me of giving her attitudes. Therefore, that was the third time lawyers had been changed for the court case.

The same lady who represented the Judge in room ###, told her in front me behind close door that there was a stipulation of agreement. I let the new lawyer knew that one of the roommates (Sub-landlord) left since end of April 2018. I let the new lawyer knew behind close door, in front of the lady who represented the Judge, that $200 that her client(s) claimed I owed was false and her client(s) added $50 every ten days on that $200. I let the lawyer knew that her client(s) done that to everyone who rented apartments or rooms from them on wrong charges. I said that this would be the second time that will be evicted illegally. I saw both of them gave this kind of strange look. The third lawyer called her law firm to report about the stipulation of agreement. She said to the lady who represented the Judge that her law firm did not do anything like that. The second lawyer who created the stipulation of agreement had to come to courtroom ###. Few minutes later, the courtroom held only the court case and we faced the Judge. The lawyer accused by saying that it was me playing games and I should get blame for everything. I let the Judge knew about that ### Prospect place was not existed. I showed the Judge the picture I took as evidence. I found that the lawyer was trying to get himself out of that stipulation of agreement; by making it looked like he was not the one who wrote it. The Judge reminded the lawyer that he was the one who created stipulation of agreement and he should be held responsible and accountable for it.

I gave the Judge the records of the texting and read it in front of everyone in the courtroom (me, the lawyer, court officer, and the person who worked for the Judge). I gave the Judge the record of the email. The Judge said that he had a lot to read in other court cases. The Judge started to look the front and I told him to look before the last page. I was trying to make the lawyer to remember that I had to force him to add information about the addresses of the buildings and the full names of the landlord. I raised my finger while the Judge talked with a little anger toward the lawyer, and the Judge raised one of his fingers as a signal to stop, do not get involve. The Judge said to the lawyer that the landlord must come to court on 9/20/18 at 9am. I asked the Judge permission if I could work some hours in the morning and come to court at 2pm. The Judge replied no problem. When I came back to court on **9/20/18**, I did not know if I was back again in courtroom ###, instead of courtroom ###. The courtroom ### was locked when I came in, and I decided to check my name on the list of courtroom ###. I found out that I was on the list and the court case happened to be the last court case on the list at 9:30am. I spoke to the gentleman who represented the Judge in courtroom ### about the court time as everyone got in courtroom ###, at about 2:30pm. The gentleman told me to sit down, he would check it out. Few minutes later the gentleman called my name and told me that the court time changed for 2pm. The gentleman also told me to go sit down waiting for the Judge.

The case turned out to be called first in front of the Judge after lunch. The second lawyer was there and changed what had been said in courtroom ### that #### Bedford Avenue is ### and ### Prospect Place, even though it was not included on the stipulation of agreement. The Judge did not care about what I showed the other Judge on my as evidence that ### Prospect place was not existed. That also counts as another major problems and issues which led to perjury. The Judge said that the case was mine and wrote his decision on paper. The second lawyer walked out of the courtroom with a smile on his face, while the Judge wrote his decision. The Judge did something that he never did while I had been in court handled other cases in courtroom ###. The Judge read his decision out loud so that everyone could hear. The fourth lawyer picked up the copy of that decision. I also did not know that if the case had a different lawyer again. The fourth lawyer asked if I had the copy of the bill. I replied yes, I had it, and there was no need to give it to me.

One 10/18/18, I received another marshal notice that sent out on 10/10/18. I received the notice very late due to the wrong zip code that it was sent on purpose. I also received the notice to pick up at the post office which had date of 10/16/18 on it. I decided to go to the post office on 10/19/18 to pick up the letter. The letter turned out to be the same marshal notice sent to me on the same date (10/10/18) certified mail. I went to court on 10/23/18 at 9am. I was on the second floor filled out papers. I have been told to go to courtroom ### (HP action) about 30 minutes later. I sat there and the lawyer who worked for the Judge in the courtroom called in behind close door. He did not give me advised at all about what I should do when I asked him. I tried to make transition of the case with what had been happened on 9/29/14. The court did not allow me to do that. The lawyer already knew it would be denied by the Judge. The lawyer said that the case had reached it ends. The lawyer also sent me in appellate on 15th floor when he also knew that the appeal would be denied. I went out make copies since it is expensive to make copies on the second floor where they gave the court file to make copies of what I needed to do the appeal. It costed 25 cent per copy. I have been told that could not go out with the court file. I was lucky that I had the original of few documents. I gave back the court file and went out to make copies. I came back to court around two o'clock. I went straight to the 15th floor and sat there for about one hour and half. The appeal had been denial by the Judge on that floor, which I already knew that was going to happen and a waste of my time. I left court at about 3:30pm that day.

I was out of town on **10/27/18** and came back on **10/31/18** at about 9:30 pm and found the marshal eviction was at the door and the lock changed. I called the landlord right away and sent him a text. I called him early in the morning on the next day (11/1/18). The landlord finally picked up and told me to call the super. I asked him about the super phone number. He gave it to me without given me the super name, and hung up on me right away. I called the super more than twice that morning. I even called S**** and told me to keep calling the super. I sent text to the super. He texted me back about 30 minutes later with new information about the new management. The new management is G******** M********. I called them few times and decided to call me back. The gentleman who called me back told me that he believed that my belonging had been throwing out. He told me that he would call me back. He never did call me back, but only I called few times. A lady called me back and told me that someone will meet with to get my belongings. I met with the super in front of the building. His name is M* (or M**). When I got in the apartment around 12pm and found only two bags of trash. One of them was in the roommate's room which spent the same amount as me per month and the other one was by the entrance. I found most of the rest of my belongings had been throwing out and few might be stolen. what might be stolen are my over $100 worth of quarter collections, over $ 50 of my special pillow, blender cost about $60, two fleeces of bed sheet (King sizes) about $50, one quilt of bed sheet $ 20, over $50 St. Crawford umbrella, HD antenna that was in the box of PlayStation about $ 45, dishes, and $ 30 worth of water filter plastic container, shaving razors in the small toilet bottom draw along with two bars of soap, over $30 of Klear Kanteen 64(oz), and almost $20 of Walt Disney cup. The biggest amount of over $ 370 of my credit card bill that I prepared to send had been lost or stolen. It was locked in my room either on the bed sheet I was sleeping on, or on the box next to the bed sheet. Some of my documents that were in two white plastic bags were also throwing out as trash. I also lost or missing about $45n dollars' worth of groceries. I found it strange that no one called me and told me that I was evicted illegally and I need to get the rest of my belongings out. They had my email and phone number. The room I was in was locked. These people went into the room, by removing the lock, and did whatever they wanted. I decided to go back to court along with the copy of the marshal eviction at 2:30pm. I was on the second floor filed paperwork and sent in courtroom 407. The court clerk told me that I must fill out the paper work if I wanted to go back to the apartment. The court clerk told me that someone is not doing something right and I wonder who. It seems to me that the law firm and the client evicted due to removal and demolition. I was in the apartment to get the remaining of my belongings, and there was no demolition going but polishing everything and ready to rent the apartment again. The gentleman who worked for the Judge in courtroom ### said to go serve the lawyer in room ### (the lawyers' office) to be in court on 11/5/18. The second lawyer was in room ### and laugh when I served the paper. He told me that I should have left already.

One **11/5/18** at approximately 10:20am in courtroom ###, a fifth lawyer called out my name and brought me out of the courtroom. I did not listen to what he had to say, but only told him to go f*** himself. I faced the Judge shortly, about five minutes later. The lawyer placed a paper on the table below and wondered if he gave the same paper to the court. The Judge told me about the decision that he made on paper in October 2018 that I should vacate with dignity. I let the Judge knew that I was evicted on the wrong zip code which led to perjury. The judge replied that there was no perjury going one there. I raised the paper high enough for the Judge and everyone else to see and told the lawyer that he gave me that paper when the case is already done. I let the Judge knew that I lost about $700 worth of belongings. I picked up my belonging that was on the table behind me and I pointed my finger to the lawyer and said I am coming after his f***ing company (referred to his law firm). The court officer was there and followed me out and slightly pushed me against the wall out of the courtroom and told me that I was in no position to make that statement. All I could say was to say sorry three times. I was lucky enough to have my personal record of what had been going on throughout the case. I hope that the court had audios available. The reason why that is there are lies, problems, and false allegation that the law firm had against as their defense. The law firm and their clients had been committed corruption, extortion, robbery, perjury, slavery, lies, denial, manifesto of racial prejudice, and pretention, going on throughout the case. The law firm never mentioned any of them on their defense, but simply playing innocent. I sent the copy of their defense along with my notes on them, particularly about what I knew going on in the case. The court should also get blame and contribute to the problem. The court and the law firm made me waste my time and I was still evicted illegally without protection. This is the second time I evicted and the court had double my criminal record on that, and unable more to apply for apartment and job. Who is going to pay for messing up my life twice in the housing issues and problems? I am into this mess because of the court even though the court does not want to admit it. Who wants to be in the problem that I am in? That is not my problem when lawyers and their clients continue not having respect for the court, particularly when they go against the Judge's decision to evict me illegally twice. These lawyers and clients continue to take the court as joke and destroy tenants' live politically, socially, and economically.

I send the court summaries of both cases to the Justice Department (case index # holdover proceeding & # claim). I am currently with my uncle and hope that everything workout before my uncle lose his apartment real soon. The landlord never fixed the apartment. All they did was hiding problems with paint on October 2018. He was in court back in 2013 over the maintenance issues. The apartment is getting worse. I will be evicted illegally if anything happens in the future on **"JOHN DOE and JANE DOE"**, Just like in the previous case. The lawyers and their clients would do whatever they want and the court would never take strong action against them. Therefore, I will be the one suffer the consequence of everyone's wrongdoing. I could not go back to the shelter for two reasons. The first reason is that the shelter is filthy and do not want to attract any disease. The second reason is that I do not want to go live with roommates who may have been lunatics and do not pay their fair share on rent and utilities. I will find myself come back to court again on the same problems and issues of corruption, extortion, robbery, lies, pretention, discrimination, prejudice, and injustice done by the landlords' lawyer(s) and the landlords. I will waste my time to come in court more than six times. I will also waste my time to have my response prepare and not collect or ignore by the court. That would also affect my job when I have to be in court many times and have all of my time waste for no reason at all.

Note: I remember one day on October 2018, probably first or second week of October I came from work, the lady who lives below me told me that the manager told her that I should have left the apartment already. I responded by saying to her that why should I leave when they collected the October rent from me. I asked the lady if she got the name of the manager. She responded, no. The conversation took place at the lobby.

Note: All of the first three lawyers, particularly the first two lawyers, told me that I should not be in court. I found that strange, confuse, and overwhelm. My name and the others were in record to show up in court. I am under suspicion that all of us would get affected if the roommate (sub-landlord) whom the landlord and the others dropped the responsibility on and accused the rest of us that we should have been in court no matter what. We would end up evicted without court date and trial. I was lucky enough to listen to one of the tenants on the second floor told me to go to court immediately, when I received the court paper. The tenant even told me that they tried to bribe him with $ 50,000 dollars to get out of the building. That tenant is a concerned tenant; he told me that I should send report to the (authority name omitted) about the building when I mentioned that to him. He told me that the court would never do anything about the entire problem that had been going on in the building.

Note: I do not mind to leave the place due to ridiculous charges on rent which leads to corruption, extortion, and robbery. The building is filthy and infested by roaches, mice and rats. That was what I witness few days later, after I left court in June 2018. I witnessed a huge rat had it butt cheek stuck on a mice trap and managed to set itself free by fleeing under the heater by the entrance. The rat got away to some degree because of me. I went to my room to get the mop stick to slay the rat. I place my foot on the mice trap while the rat was already under the heater. Therefore the rat got away. I want to go back where I was evicted illegally. It is the court that keeps me homeless and does not want to take full responsibility of destroying my life to some degree. The place is also noisy 24/7, on the street and in the apartment above me. The landlord and the other did not repair the apartments well and the ceiling could collapse on anyone in the future. That already happened in the apartment across me.

Note: On the day that the landlord called me while I was at work, he said that he was helping me. I added to the conversation by saying to the landlord that he was not living way in the past where he could get away with problems and lies that he and the others committed. Otherwise I may be mistaken; the past of that time is still remained in modern life and/or society.

Note: send to Authority

Note: almost ignore by the court

Van Hugo <Van####@yahoo.com>
To: R***** M
Apr 20, 2018 at 12:59 PM

To R*****

You are saying that the others are out, and I may be the only one who will stay to pay $3050 per month by myself. I need an answer.

Van Hugo

On Friday, April 20, 2018, 11:24:11 AM EDT, Rachel M
<r*****@a**y******.com> wrote:

Van,

We can not re-new the lease agreement, there is large balance on the apartment that needs to be paid and we can rent one room. The monthly rent is $3050, with our approval requirements you can not afford to hold this lease and pay the balance.

Please confirm times brokers can show the space. Ty

Van Hugo

On Wed, Apr 18, 2018 at 11:06 PM, Van Hugo <Van####@yahoo.com> wrote:

To R*****

I send this email to find out if I can extend the date to move out. I am in the process of looking for other place. It is sudden to move out. Otherwise you should find me another place.

Van Hugo

On Wednesday, April 18, 2018, 3:52:50 PM EDT, Rachel M <r*****@ally******.com> wrote:

Hello,

You are receiving this email because you have given notice that you may not be renewing you're lease agreement.

To begin working on the move out process please note that we need to begin showing your apartment and coordinating access for our brokerage companies.

Please respond to this email with a point of contact and times weekly and on the weekends that would work for you (roommates) for our brokerage companies to show.

This email will be a basis for us to communicate to ensure there is routine access for both parties.

Please note for a return of you're security deposit you will need to email securitydepost@ally******.com after you have coordinated a walk through with you're super.

As a reminder the move out date for you're apartment is 05.31.2018 by midnight no later, the apartment keys must be returned by that time to ensure a full refund of you're deposit.

-- R*****

All Y*** M*********

Hand written note: "A** Y**** M********* is affiliated with R**** P****** R*****LLC"

Note: send to Authority

Note: ignore by court and law firm

R**** P****** R*****LLC   R**** P****** R*****LLC

Lee ave suite (box) ####   ### Lee ave suite (box)

Bk NY 112##   BK NY 112##

7/6/17

To P****** R**** R***** LLC

 I send this letter on the behalf of management or owner of P****** R**** Realty LLC concerning about the June 2017 rent payment of $775 dollars I made by money order, for the room I rent at #### Pacific street unit #. I never get any full address to endorse money to the place from the real estate that helped get the place or the management of the company. The agent of the real estate I met told me to send money to R**** P****** Realty LLC without gave the borough and zip code of the place. I did ask for it and never gave it to me. I checked only and found only P****** R**** R***** LLC located at ### Lee avenue Suite #### Bk NY #####. I began to face problem from someone by the name D***. I told that person I need what train goes to the address. D*** told me the G train goes to near the address. D*** told me that she or he would live at 5pm. It was already too late not only the place was far from the address, but also look for the place. I got there nearly 5:30 pm and found out it place of mailboxes. I assume that Suite #### is box ####. I sent email to explain everything to D*** and still blame me for something that was not my fault to begin with. He told me I should endorse money order or check to "all y*** m*********" LLC" at the same address suite ***, which is box ***. If any of you affiliated with "all y*** m*********", send me back the money order on the addresses indicate below. I suggest that the money order sent to my P.O. Box ### bk NY #####. Even D*** said it does not matter which management I sent the money because they are the same company by email. I hope to hear from anyone of you.

I want all of you to know that what you did to me is unfair and unacceptable. All of seemed to blame me for something that was not my fault. I only get information from the agent about sending money order to "R**** P****** Realty LLC", without giving me the full address. I did ask him about it, but he never replied to my email. The agent never mentioned anything about "all y*** m*********" to me. I went to the place on 7/3/17 at approximately 5:25 pm to drop the money order at ### Lee ave bk NY #####. I went to the place at approximately 5:20 pm trying to get the envelope I placed the money order. I found out from the employee that helped me out that the envelope had been picked up early after he checked the box I dropped the envelope in and the box ####. He asked my full name and phone number in case if he received the envelope. I told him that he could drop in box ###, otherwise called me if he wanted me to come to pick up the envelope. There is camera (s) in the place to prove everything. He was shocked when I showed him proof of the name of the places and the place had two different box numbers. He wondered if both places affiliated to each other. The employee told me that he knew the person for box ####.

I send everything that I found to both addresses and boxes to all of you. Doing so is a way that none of you would say that you did not know, even though all of you seemed to know but pretend that you did not know. I also want to know all of your full names and the full names of the landlord (s). All of you know about me; particularly invaded to my privacy to get a room. I want you to know that I cannot pay the amount of $775 a month in my credit card due to the limits I have on it. That amount you ask me to pay per month will affect other payments and purchase on my credit card. As for my bank account, forget about it. I want to know why payment with money order seems to be problem or issue here.

Sincerely

Van Hugo

Van Hugo
Email address omitted
Phone number omitted

Note: send to Authority

Note: ignored by court and law firm

5/12/18

Van Hugo

Pacific St apt
bk, ny, #####

I send this letter to let you know that your clients have committed not extortion, corruption, and robbery. Your clients have been harassing me to pay money that I do not owe. Your clients want me to pay money for those who are owe and stated that it is their policies and it is on the Proprietary Lease to which I never get any copy of. I have been on the issues with your clients since the day I moved in the apartment and room. I also want you to know that one of us moved out of the apartment and room at the end of April 2018. I send this letter along with the last emails i sent to you clients in the mid of April. I also send it to you with some of the emails that your clients send to me. I want you to know that your clients gave us until 5/31/18 to leave the apartment. I found it absurd of your clients to try to get lawyers. You better read it carefully because I sent a lot to your clients last year. Your clients evict me without bringing me to court. Your clients make it look like it is not an eviction.

Sincerely

Van Hugo

Jericho Turnpike
New Hyde, Park, NY, #####

Note: send to Authority

Note: ignored by court and law firm

4/21/18

From Van Hugo

To R***** and all (M****, L***, Y****, and the other roommates by email)

Send to G*****, M****, B**** & S********* on 5/12/18 (### Jericho Turnpike, New Hyde Park NY #####)

Note: All Y*** M********* affiliated with P****** R**** Realty LLC at ### Lee Ave BK NY #####

Note: D*** also knows about what is going on

Since you do not respond to my last email, I want you to know that there are some issues at play there.

The first sets of issues are about the affordability of the apartment. I have paper stated that I should pay $775 per month for the apartment. That never included the room. Paying $3050 dollars for the apartment, considered a huge crime leads to corruption, extortion, and robbery. No one would pay for that amount a month in this place whether they have money. I would like to know how much you and the others pay for the places that you all live in. I would not be surprised if any of you do not pay anything for over twenty or thirty years. The money that I heard that I owed is a bogus charge against me.

The second sets of issues are that I went to the shelter for help on 4/ 19/ 18 right after work. I spend nearly 5 hours in the place for no reason because of all of you caused problem for me. I have been interviewed and interrogated by them. They asked me to bring information about the building. This information had to do about the address of the place and the name of the Landlord. They also asked me to bring the Proprietary Lease to which I never got any copy of when I came to the apartment last year (2017). They even told me that how can I evicted when I have not being bringing in court. They keep my case on pending since I gave them the date that all of you asked me to leave the apartment.

The third sets of issues are that if you happen to bring me in court the address to serve me is (P.O. Box ### Bk, NY, #####). if there is a problem, let me know otherwise serve me on the building's address even though the mail box of the apartment happens to be the only mail box that is not even protect and secure, because anyone can open it and steal anything there, as well as invade in my and the others privacies. I have been in the housing court before; do not try any funny business. I do not think any lawyers in the City would take your cases, unless they dumb and stupid to take it. I would go more after them to trap everyone with that lawyer. If you are going to hire G******* & L****** PLLC and LLP, the case would get worse. I have cases against them for committed perjury, falsified information & documents, and Identity theft. The law firm and their clients had to bear not my problems, issues, and responsibilities, but also the whole building as well. The lawyer(s) and their clients evicted me by going against the Judge's decision. It is the lawyers that the Judge asked me to go serve. I even make things worst not on for them, but also for the Court as well which let me abandoned and neglected on my case, by sending all of my reports to the (authority name omitted). I hope things would not get that far. If all of you still want to take action against me by bringing me in court, you can either have a holdover proceeding against me or money on rent. You cannot do both.

The fourth sets of issues are that the Super and all of you have the key to the apartment. What I am under suspicion of what is going to happen is that on 5/31/18, someone will come in and change the lock without of our knowledge. That happened before when I brought my belonging in the apartment on 5/27/17. No one called me to tell me about that and I ended charged for days I did not spend in the apartment. The date I should move included on the paper that I received after I made all of the full payment ($775 for deposit & $775 for rent). I moved in on 6/2/17. The rent for that period was from end or close to end of May 2017 until end of June 2017. I knew there would be problem with that anyway.

I want all of you to know that problems could avoid. I want to live in peace until my problem resolved. I do not care about the kind of business that all of you are conducted in this building. All I see all of you are doing is to drag me into problem while pretending you are not doing so. The choice is yours and I will begin to move most of my stuff out at this moment.

Van Hugo
Email address omitted
Phone number omitted

Van Hugo
Pacific st apt
Bk, NY, #####

P.O. Box ###
BK NY #####

Note: send to Authority

Note: Ignored by the court

Report written by Van Hugo from 5/27/18 to 5/30/18
Index #: omitted

There are other issues and problems that the building and the apartments face. The Landlord of the building does not do good work in the building. All the Landlord does is to hide problems in the building by using paint and other materials to do so. That was what had been going on, after the incident that occurred in the apartment across me (apt #).

The ceiling of the apartment collapsed on the tenants (or roommates) on the weekend of 4/21/18 or 4/22/18, in the morning. I never see them come back in the apartment ever since the incident happened. It seemed to be that the response and/or the incident that happened caused the Landlord of the building to do some patching work in the building and the apartment. It is also too risky for me to live in the room and apartment because there was not any good work done in the apartment. The only part of the apartment that looks fine is only the bathroom and restroom. Some of the woods in my room are moving under my feet, as well as some of the woods in the hallway near what appears to be the kitchen. Rain somehow finds its way in my room when it is pouring out. Sometimes, I hear huge noises through the ceiling of my room, by the windows. It seems to be that pieces of cement fallen apart through the ceiling. The neighbors above me not only making noises every day, but also seems to nail some woods that appear to come off the floor. The whole building and the apartments are hollow.

The place that sent me to the building (realty name omitted) does not care about what happened to me. I have been contacted them when the Landlord or Management of the building said I owed money, on the day I moved in until now. They said that it is out of their hands, and left me alone with the problems. I even told the agents of the Landlord to bring me in court last year (2017). Another person by the name D***, threaten the others and I about bringing us to court before. It is absurd of the Landlord or agents of the Landlord to bring me in court late. They asked the others and I to leave the apartment on 5/31/18. They served us late (nearly on the middle of May 2018). One of us left maybe on the last Thursday going on Friday of April 2018. The other one left probably beginning of May 2018. It seemed to be that the Landlord or Management charges them for May 2018 rent. Therefore, the Landlord brings them in court without their knowledge. The Landlord or agents of the Landlord use their policy and lease against me. M**** said that on one of the email that he sent to the others and I that the Landlord said that he or she is not going to renew the lease to all of us anymore (middle of April 2018). M**** also said that the Landlord wanted us to leave by 5/31/18. Rachel said that I could not afford to pay the whole $3050 a month on rent. The Landlord or the agents of the Landlord want me to pay the whole amount that the some of us owed, along with $3050 on monthly rent. The Landlord or the agents of the Landlord want me to pay $3050 per month for the apartment, along with the other empty three rooms. I happened to be the only one who sent the renewal form of the lease three times. What happened to me is not only based on corruption, extortion, and robbery, but also all the prejudice, discrimination, and injustice that come along with them. It is wrong and immoral to pay the debt of somebody else, when I do not owe anything. What happen to me also done on purpose?

I have been into this position and problem because of the court. I have been evicted on September 29, 2014 illegally. I do not know what is going with the appeal that I file. The Judge who held the trial of the Holdover Proceeding seems to care less about my case. The Person I chose on the list that the Court gave me to do the appeal (Private Company) also seems to care less about my case. I reach out to them by writing and phone calls many times, but they never reply. All I get is blame me that I did not do anything, when I came to court wandering around looking for some answers. My case number is (omitted). The problem that the illegal eviction caused to me is to prevent me from getting apartments out there. The court gave me a criminal record as a result. I could not apply for any decent job, particularly government jobs now, due to the reason that I have been dislocated and homeless for nearly four years and a half. Therefore, the court gives me a criminal record for no reason. The court should know that the manifesto of racial prejudice is remaining towards people of color, particularly African American, to some degree. The court has left me on my own without any protection. It is also absurd of the court to ask me to do an appeal when I actually do not have a physical address. I did the best I could to get an address to do the appeal. However, I was unable to stay there and I left.

Added after I left court on June 1, 2018

There is one option that the court must choose from out of the three options. The first option is that I want to go back to the primary address (the address I was evicted from on September 29, 2014) effective immediately. I never use the #### pacific street as my primary address. Most of the roommates did the same thing. The second option is that the court must pay the whole amount that the Landlord wants me to pay on late fees, owed on rent, and monthly rent. Otherwise, I will pay the $775 per month for the room I rent and the court will pay the remaining. The third option is that I stay in the apartment and pay what I pay per month for my room until the court brings me back to the apartment I was evicted from illegally on September 29, 2014. There are two reasons why I give the court to choose one option out of the three options. The first reason is that the person who represents the court did not collect my documents and exhibits behind close door. The second reason is that the person who represents the court seemed to agree at what the landlord's lawyer said about to pay the whole $3050, along with the fees of over $8000 or $9000 that the other roommates owed.

*Hand written note: On July 10, 2018, someone by the name **S** G**, told me over the phone that I should have left the apartment on July 5, 2018. I found that prejudice, discrimination, and injustice because I paid this month rent. He said that he is the manager.*

Note: send to Authority

Text: Collected in Court

8/1/18 5:00pm

To A** F*****: I send this text to let you know that I called you twice and no one called me back to meet at the two addresses I should meet with, to see the apartments. If it is not happening today (8/1/18), you have until the time that your lawyer stated on paper. I will pay this month rent at the current address. If I could meet with anyone at your inconvenience today, I will be available to meet with them at my schedule. I will be available at 5:30pm from Monday to Friday, and in the morning and afternoon on the weekends.

Van Hugo

Van Hugo

8/1/18 6:36pm

A**: Please call her ##########

8/1/18 6:46pm

A**: S*** trying to call you

To S*** 8/2/18

I want you to know that there was an agreement to see two apartments (### and ### Prospect place). You either send me a text or email at <u>(email address omitted)</u> to set up an appointment. I told Abe F***** by texting of days available for that. I will be available at 5:30pm from Monday to Friday. I will be available in the morning or afternoon on the weekends, particularly on Saturday. I should see these two rooms the same day of the appointment.

Van Hugo

8/2/18 10:48am

S***: ok thank you.

8/3/18 4:53pm

To S***

I want you to know that I really want to meet with you as soon as possible because I will be on vacation from 8/20/18 to 8/27/18 and I will not be around to meet with you on these days.

Van Hugo

8/3/18 5:13pm

S***: yes we will be meeting tomorrow.

8/3/18 7:50pm

To S***

I send you a last text as a reminder to get the address, the time, and train I should get off to meet with you tomorrow (Saturday).

Van Hugo

8/4/18 9:36am

S***: good morning, what time is best for you today?

8/4/18 9:50am

To S***

What time is best for you today?

S***: working on it with the weather now. I think around 2 would work for everyone.

8/4/18 10:04 am

To S***

I assume you mean 2pm. One more time send me the address and what train I should take for the meet.

Van Hugo

Van Hugo

S***: the agent called you to show you the room.

To Shee

I want to you to know why you have M****** from the real estate calling me and do something different other than what we have agreed in court. #### Dean st was not part of the agreement.

Van Hugo

S***: the other room we have is $975 and M****** works with us as a broker. #### Dean has a room in your price point and will work for you. If you want to wait until Abe come back online ok.

To S***

That you and A** responsibility. You guys talk it over. I am waiting of what has been promised to me.

Note: send to Authority

Email record: Collected in Court

On Wednesday, August 15, 2018, 12:44:51 PM EDT, L*** <l***@a**y***m**.com> wrote:

Hi

Did you view the apartment at ### Prospect pl yesterday?

Please note I am in the office Monday thru Thursday 10:00- 4:00, Friday 10:00 12:00. (No actual office, but lies about it)

Van Hugo <Van####@yahoo.com>
To: L***
Aug 15 at 1:19 PM

To l***

No one sent me email or text about that. ### or ### prospect place is the agreement. I have to choose one. #### dean street was not the agreement. S*** and A** told me that ### and ### prospect place are not available anymore early this month. I never heard from them ever since, until you send me this email. I will not be available from 8/20/18 to 8/27/18 because of vacation. S*** and A** knew about that.

Van Hugo

On Wednesday, August 15, 2018, 1:58:38 PM EDT, L*** <l***@a**y***m**.com> wrote:

Hi

Prospect Pl # 2L you can view on Friday Between 8:00 and 11:00, however the rent over there is $920. Will you be there at that time to view the apartment?

Please note I am in the office Monday thru Thursday 10:00- 4:00, Friday 10:00 12:00.

(No actual office, but lies about it)

Van Hugo <Van####@yahoo.com>
To: L***
Aug 15 at 2:10 PM

To L***

I have been told the same thing. However, why A** agreed in court stated that I will pay the same amount I paid at #### Pacific st in ### or ### Prospect place. It seems to me that A** lied. How this is going to look court.

Van Hugo

Van Hugo

On Wednesday, August 15, 2018, 2:27:56 PM EDT, L*** <l***@a**y***m**.com> wrote:

Hi

Ok, first please look at it to see if it fits your need and we will talk about the rent afterwards.

Thank You

Please note I am in the office Monday thru Thursday 10:00- 4:00, Friday 10:00 12:00.

(No actual office, but lies about it)

Van Hugo <Van####@yahoo.com>
To: L***
Aug 15 at 2:39 PM

To L***

I do not mind to look at it. As i said before which you tried to ignore is that i have to look at two apartments on each address (*** and *** prospect place) and choose one. I need to do that the same day. As for the rent, there will be nothing to discuss about. I will continue to pay what i pay at **** pacific st ($775 per month). Paying less than what that will be grateful.

Van Hugo

On Wednesday, August 15, 2018, 4:00:34 PM EDT, L*** <l***@a**y***m**.com> wrote:

Hi

You need to understand that these are occupied apartments and times need to be facilitated with the tenants. We can not promise to see both apartments the same day. You will need to look at it when the roommates are home (in no place in the stip it stated that it needs to be in the same date).

Please note I am in the office Monday thru Thursday 10:00- 4:00, Friday 10:00 12:00.

(No actual office, but lies about it)

Van Hugo <Van####@yahoo.com>
To: L***
Aug 15 at 5:33 PM

To l***

I need to see both of them at the same time. Time is short for me because of all of you. I have been trying to get things done early as soon as i leave court this month. Therefore the problem come from all of you. There is no guarantee that i will not come back to court over the same problem about held responsible and accountable unfairly about someone depth. It is like i move from one problem to a potential problem in the future. You make rhe appointment happen for both apartments and i will be waiting.

Van Hugo

Van Hugo <Van####@yahoo.com>
To: L***
Aug 16 at 10:27 AM

To L***

I want you to know this is the agreement to see both apartments the same day. That was what stated in court paper. These addresses located on the same street. One more thing, i wonder why you and the others always drop your responsibilities to the tenants or roommates. The court papers never

Van Hugo

indicated that tenants or roommates to show me the apartments or rooms. It is still going against what the landlord and his lawyer wrote on paper.

Van Hugo

On Thursday, August 16, 2018, 4:22:38 PM EDT, L*** <l***@a**y***m**. com> wrote:

Hi

I just want to confirm that you will be tomorrow at *** 2L between 8:00-11:00 to view the apartment to see if it is a fit for you.

Thank You

Please note I am in the office Monday thru Thursday 10:00- 4:00, Friday 10:00 12:00.

(No actual office, but lies about it)

Van Hugo <Van####@yahoo.com>
To: L***
Aug 16 at 5:15 PM

To L***

I want to know is it 8:00-11:00 in the morning or afternoon. I won't be able to make it in the morning because of work. I already give the time that i am available. I am available at 5:30pm after work. I would have to see both *** and *** prospect place the same day.

Van Hugo

On Friday, August 17, 2018, 10:01:14 AM EDT, L*** <l***@a**y***m**. com> wrote:

As explained previously those are occupied apartments, in order to see it you need to work with the current tenants schedules.

Please note I am in the office Monday thru Thursday 10:00- 4:00, Friday 10:00 12:00.

(No actual office, but lies about it)

Van Hugo <Van####@yahoo.com>
To: L***
Aug 17 at 10:12 AM

To L***

I want you to know one more time it is you and the others responsibilities the make that happened. I have until today to make that happen. I will not be around tomorrow until 8/27/18. I should not be around after work today. It you and the others who failed to take your responsibility appropriately, properly, and effectively. One more thing some body by the name E**** sent me a text around 7pm and she never replied to my text. Who is she a roommate or real estate? She stated that R***** told her I have been looking for a room.

Van Hugo

On Friday, August 17, 2018, 12:03:08 PM EDT, L*** <l***@a**y***m**.com> wrote:

Hi

She is the tenant in #### (Bedford ave) and she can show you that room. It is not our responsibility that you are going on vacation. We are willing to show you that apartments and have offered you to show other apartments as well which you denied for no good reason.

Please note I am in the office Monday thru Thursday 10:00- 4:00, Friday 10:00 12:00.

(No actual office, but lies about it)

Van Hugo <Van####@yahoo.com>
To: L***
Aug 17 at 5:10 PM

To L*** (resend)

It is my responsibility. It is not my responsibility that you and the others playing stupid games, particularly the landlord who used Jewish holiday on July 13, 2018 as an excuse, pretext, and advantage not to show up in court. I wanted everything to be done two months ago in court. All of make me go to court 3 times for no reason and changed lawyers. Its your responsibility that you and the other remaining careless, arrogant, and ignorant, irresponsible in everything that has been going on. The court paper stated that by August 7, 2018 I should find anything by now on ### or ### Prospect place. All of you have been messing up my schedule for months. Who's fault is it? Of course it is, I am always going to be the victim and patsy (scapegoat) to you and everybody else's failure. All of you had been doing is that to blame for all of the problems that you have been created, to commit corruption, extortion, and robbery. I warned all of you from the beginning just to leave me alone. Your arrogance and ignorance got the best of all of you. You accuse me saying that you are helping and denied apartments for no good reason. That can be used against you in a court of law because all of you and the others are doing is to go against your agreements that stated in court document. One thing, be clear and specific about E****'s address. #### what (Dean st, Prospect Place).

Van Hugo

Van Hugo <Van####@yahoo.com>
To: L***
Aug 20 at 3:04 PM

To L***

**** Bedford was not part of the deal and agreement. As I said before, I am currently out of town until 8/27/18 on the afternoon.

Skarov Masson

On Monday, August 20, 2018, 10:51:02 AM EDT, L*** <l***@a**y***m**.com> wrote:

Hi

Sorry if I was not clear with E****'s Address it is *** Prospect pl/**** Bedford (it is a corner building). We have a room available there so please get back to here so you can view it.

Van Hugo <Van####@yahoo.com>
To: L***
Aug 20 at 4:02 PM

To L***

Still, it is not part of the agreement.

Van Hugo

On Monday, August 20, 2018, 3:23:01 PM EDT, L*** <l***@a**y***m**.com> wrote:

Please read my email again ### Prospect pl is #### Bedford it is a corner building.

On Tuesday, August 21, 2018, 10:16:10 AM EDT, L*** <l***@a**y***m**. com> wrote:

Yes it is.

Van Hugo <Van####@yahoo.com>
To: L***
Aug 21 at 3:02 PM

To L***

You and the others have to bring that in court. Stop wasting my time.

Van Hugo

Note: send to Authority, not this extended version. Authority received it along with the hand writing on it.

Note: I only sent response to what I know going on.

Extended Version

Law firm defense 3: I submit this affirmation in opposition to Respondent, my name omitted post-eviction order to show cause to be restored to possession to the premises based upon the Respondent's failure to comply with the August 1, 208 So-Ordered stipulation of settlement and Decision and Order dated September 20, 2018.

My response to defense 3: not true, I complied with the stipulation of agreement, but being screwed by the law firm and its clients. The question is who wrote the stipulation of agreement (the law firm or landlord).

Law firm defense 4: Respondent currently makes this post-eviction application, yet falis to establish that he has the funds available to make the Landlord whole since execution of the warrant of eviction was stayed for the Respondent to vacate and conditioned waiving all arrears on timely vacatur. In fact, Respondent failed to attach any proof whatsoever that he can pay off the arrears, marshal's fees, legal fees and ongoing rent.

My response to defense 4: I only pay for my room. I have no other rooms under my responsibilities. I did brought proof, but ignored by the court or Judges in courtroom ###, & ###. Only few Proofs collected in court and reviewed to some degree.

Law firm defense 5: A review of the history of this proceeding shows that the Respondent has continuously defaulted on his obligation to pay the rent for the subject premises. Respondent is either unable or unwilling to provide proof of his present ability to pay the arrears due, or his ability to pay the ongoing rent that will continue to come due. Therefore, the Respondent should not be granted a further extension of time given the long duration of this proceeding and the ample opportunity that has already been provided to the Respondent.

My response to defense 5: I only pay for my room ($775 per month).

Law firm defense 6: This nonpayment proceeding was commenced based upon the Respondent's failure to pay rent on a timely basis for the property located at #### Pacific street, Apt #, Brooklyn, NY, wrong zip code (hereinafter "subject premises") pursuant to a Notice of Petition and Petition after service of a rent demand.

My response to defense 6: Serve on the wrong zip code on purpose by the law firm and its clients which led to perjury.

Law firm defense 7: Upon information and belief, the Respondent thereafter submitted an Answer to the instant proceeding and the case was first before this court on June 1, 2018.

My respondent to defense 7: The same answer I sent to the law firm and its client before court date was ignore behind closed door. The first lawyer showed up, but trapped with the case. The landlord never showed that day.

Law firm defense 8: Upon information and belief, the parties appeared on June 1, 2018 and the proceeding was adjourned to July 13, 2018 and August 1, 2018.

My response to defense 8: The second lawyer showed up and asking for application. The landlord never showed up. The second lawyer used Jewish holiday as a cause of the landlord's absence. My response ready to collect for the first time in court, but never happened. The response ignored by the Judge in courtroom ###.

Law firm defense 9: Upon information and belief, the parties appeared on August 1, 2018, the parties appears and entered into So-Ordered stipulation of settlement whereby a final judgement was entered in favor of the Petitioner, Annexed hereto as Exhibit "1" is a copy of the August 1, 2018 So-Ordered stipulation of settlement. Execution of warrant of eviction was stayed through August 31, 2018 for the Respondent, my name omitted, to vacate from the subject premises. See Exhibit "1". Upon default, the warrant shall execute upon service of marshal's notice. See Exhibit "1". The stipulation provided that upon timely vacatur, Petitioner would waive arrears through August 2018. See Exhibit "1". The stipulation further provided that respondent could view other apartments owned by the Petitioner. Id. The proceeding was also discontinued against the other Respondents as all other tenants vacated from the subject premises.

My response to defense 9: The second lawyer and the landlord trapped with the lease. The stipulation of agreement used as a backup plan. The second lawyer knew that there was no guarantee on any promises before and after the creation of the stipulation of agreement. The second lawyer also committed prejudice and injustice towards me, which led to slavery. I was evicted illegally while the stipulation of agreement was under violation by the law firm and its clients.

Law firm defense 10: Upon information and belief, the Respondent defaulted under the August 1, 2018 So-Ordered stipulation of failing to vacate from the subject premises by August 31, 2018 and marshal's notice was served.

My response to defense 10: Wrong, the Stipulation of agreement was under violation and the second lawyer accused me of playing games. The landlord never showed in courtroom ### at approximately 2pm.

Law firm defense 11: Upon information and belief, Respondent interposed and Order to Show Cause seeking to vacate the stipulation which was returnable on September 18, 2018.

My response to defense 11: The third lawyer did not know about the stipulation of agreement and claimed that the law firm never done such thing. The third lawyer wondered why the second lawyer made stipulation of agreement when the law firm never done such thing. Otherwise the second lawyer took it upon himself to do it which under the violation of his law firm laws, rules, and/ or regulations. The lawyer may have done so because of the right, power, and privilege that he has to do things against his law firm.

Law firm defense 12: Upon information and belief, on September 18, 2018 and the proceeding was adjourned on September 20, 2018.

My response to defense 12: the forth lawyer showed up while the second lawyer walked out of the courtroom ###. The Judge unexpectedly said the case was mine and did not want to see the proof from me about that ### Prospect Place was not existed.

Law firm defense 13: Upon information and belief on September 20, 2018, this Court issued a decision and Order whereby Respondent's motion was granted to the extent that execution of the warrant was stayed through September 30, 2018 for the Respondent to pay $ 10,096.00 which represented all arrears owed through October 2018. A copy of the September 20, 2018 Decision and Order is annexed hereto as Exhibit "2". The decision and Order further noted that Petitioner complied with its obligations under the August 1, 2018 So-Ordered stipulation on the basis that the Landlord offered the Respondent other apartments. *See* Exhibit "2".

My response to defense 13: copies of the texting and emails the courtroom ### collected from me and placed them in the court file. #### Bedford avenue and #### Dean Street were not part of the agreement. How can ### and ### Prospect Place were #### Bedford avenue and #### Dean Street when no zip codes, borough, and apartment numbers were not included in the stipulation of agreement. The second lawyer had been forced by me to include them, along with the full name of the landlord and email address. The law firm and their clients never brought proof that I owed that amount. I only responsible to pay for the room I rented.

Law firm defense 17: Upon and belief, the respondent has now obtained this instant post-eviction Order to Show Cause seeking to be restored to possession. The Order to Show Cause is made returned on November 5, 2018.

My response to defense 17: the fifth lawyer laid this ridiculous paper on the table. He seemed that he is one of the head for the law firm. The law firm effectively knows that they do not have cases against me, but decided to evict under prejudice, discrimination, injustice, and under the manifesto of racial prejudice.

Law firm defense 18: The Respondent's post-eviction Order to Show Cause seeking to be restored to possession.

My response to defense 18: law firm must prove that.

Law firm defense 19: Moreover, it should be noted that the Respondent failed to attach any proof whatsoever that she can pay off the arrears, marshal's fees, legal fees and ongoing rent. Essentially, the Respondent is still in the same position as she was on the last court since she does not have enough money to cover the entire arrears balance and make the landlord whole for the legal fees and marshal's fees incurred by the landlord. Respondent had failed to state good cause to be restored to possession of the premises and this application should be denied.

My response to defense 19: are they referred to one of the roommates (sub-landlord) who left since end of April 2018 and brought her to court without her knowledge.

Law firm defense 20: Upon information and belief and according to my client's rent breakdown, the Respondent currently owes arrears through November 2018 in the amount of $ 16,496.81. *See* Exhibit "3". Upon information and belief, the Respondent also owes legal fees and Marshal's fee for the total of $1,870.13. Annexed hereto as Exhibit "4" is a copy of the legal fees billed for this account. In total the Respondent owes 18,366.94. *See* Exhibit "3" and "4".

My response to defense 20: May 24, 2017 charge was a bogus charge. The law firm and their clients knew about that. I moved in the room and apartment on June 2, 2017.

Law firm defense 21: It is imperative to note that while Respondent was lawfully evicted on or about October 29, 2018, Respondent did not attempt to be restored to possession of the subject premises until over two days after the lawful eviction on or about November 1, 2018.

My response to defense 21: the court knew that I was out of town on October 27, 2018 and came back on October 31, 2018. The eviction took place on October 29, 2018, and no one sent me a text or email about to get the rest of my belonging which most of them might be stolen. The law firm claimed that this is a lawful eviction when actually they know that I was evicted wrongfully on purpose when the law firm and their clients had no case against me. The law firm and their clients knew that I won the case and they went against the Judge's decision to evict me by forcing me out of the room and apartment.

Law firm defense 23: Moreover, it should be noted that the Respondent failed to attach any proof whatsoever that he can pay off the arrears, marshal's fees, legal fees and ongoing rent if he is restored to possession of the apartment. Essentially, the Respondent is still in the same position as he was on the last court since he does not have enough money to cover the entire arrears balance and make the landlord whole for the legal fees and marshal's fees incurred by the landlord. Respondent has failed to state the cause to be restored to possession of the premises and this application should be denied.

My response to defense 23: why should I pay these fees? I am only responsible to pay for my room.

Law firm defense 24: Even if the Respondent claims that he will pay all arrears owed as well legal fees and marshal's fees, this Court should not use their discretion to put the Respondent back into the possession of the apartment because the Respondent has continuously shown that he cannot pay ongoing rent. *See* Exhibit "1" and "3".

My response to defense 24: that is a ridiculous case.

Law firm defense 32: Moreover, the landlord will be severely injured if the Court fails to issue a stay since the Respondent has not provided a meritorious defense to this proceeding.

My response to defense 32: wrong, I did, most of them ignored by the court.

Law firm defense 33: It is imperative to not that while Respondent was lawfully evicted on or about October 29, 2018, Respondent did not take an Order to show Cause until two days after.

My response to defense 33: I was in court on October 22, 2018, in courtroom ### (HP action) which had nothing to do with the case. I have been told to go to the courtroom after I received the second marshal's eviction notice nearly a week and a half late. The second lawyer was in the courtroom pretending that he was doing something. The second lawyer saw me and pretended that he did not see me. Therefore, the law firm and their clients went against the Judge's decision and evicted me without having any proof of anything against me.

Law firm defense 34: It should be further noted that Respondent has a history of continuously failing to vacate from the apartment after receiving more time, specifically under the August 1, 2018 So-Ordered stipulation and September 20, 2018 Decision and Order. Therefore, the Respondent should not be granted a further extension of time given the long duration of this proceeding and the ample opportunity that has already been provided to the Respondent.

My response to defense 34: no proof, but only lies and false allegations against me. As I mentioned before the stipulation of agreement was a bogus and a waste of my time. There was no guarantee of anything which the law firm and their clients know about that. I have been screwed on purpose by the law firm and their clients on everything. No wonder lawyers had to change every time I came to court. I found that the law firm does not do any stipulation of agreement from the third lawyer, behind closed door. The stipulation of agreement is incomplete despite that the law firm does not do stipulation of agreement.

Law firm defense 36: Upon information and belief and according to my client's rent breakdown, the Respondent currently owes arrears through November 2018 in the amount of $16,496.81. *See* Exhibit "3". Upon information and belief, the Respondent also owes legal fees and marshal's fees of the total of $1,870.13. *See* Exhibit "4". In total, the Respondent owes $18,366.94. *See* Exhibit "3" and Exhibit "4".

My response to defense 36: what about attorney's fees. It seems that it had been omitted or excluded in the case. I wonder how much it cost to have these lawyers came to court, not doing anything effectively and charge their clients.

Law firm defense 44: In any event, if a Court decides to restore a Respondent to possession, then it must ensure that the landlord is made whole with all rent, additional rent, attorney's fees, late fees, marshal and mover's fees before the Respondent is restored to possession. NYCHA-Edenwald House V. Roque; Milton Manning; 7A Administrator V. Cecilia Nova Hernandez, N.Y. Slip Op. 4025(U) (App. Term. 1ˢᵗ Dept. May 2001); Linus Holding Corp. V. Colleen Harrison, N.Y. Slip Op. 40616 (App. Term. 1ˢᵗ Dept. Oct. 2001).

My response to defense 44: It is the tenants that are going to pay all of these fees by rent hikes unfairly. Management already charged the others and I on attorney's fees before they brought us in court. The Proprietary Lease says that the tenants must pick up the lawyer's fees whether or not the tenants are innocents.

Note: I wonder if all of these referred to me, the landlord, or the female roommate (sub-landlord) who left at the end of April 2018 and had no knowledge about coming to court. I cover my part by creating the outcome of the court case. I wonder if the law firm tries to cover itself from the problems that the attorneys and their clients put themselves into. The court also had to take blames for not collecting most of everything from me. The court made me waste my time for no reason, and knew that corruption, extortion, and robbery had been going on in the court case.

Note: this law firm exhibit 1.

Stipuplation of agreement

1) *Proceeding settled as follows: final judgment of possession entered in favor of petioner Iss and of the warrant for with execution stayed through 8/31/18 for respondent to vacate.*
2) *Petitioner agrees to two units available for viewing rental w/in 7 days which are available for move in 8/31 or earlier if the respondent agrees after inspection to take one of the units be shall be approved without application process. Address ### & ### prospect place*
3) *Conditional on timely vacatur petitioner waives all rental arrears through August 2018.*
4) *Full and timely vacatur involves leaving apartment in broom swpt condition free at all accupants and possessions items left behind shall be deemed abandoned. Keys to be surrendered to management.*
5) *Respondent agrees to contact A** F***** at (###)###-#### for viewings.*
6) *Proceeding discontinued against all other named respondents as petitioner confirms they have vacated.*

7) *Upon default petioner may execute on warrant by service at marshal's notice.*

8) *Respondent agrees to allow petitioner to show apartment upon 24 hour notice.*

Part 2

The short stories of other cases

T his is not the first time I was into stipulation of agreement. I mentioned a little about I was fired under injustice at the end of September 2016, on the previous book. I added a lot of details about that, but decided to remove it. I also mentioned about the need of the Union in the workforce to prevent employees terminated unfairly over lies under injustice. I also decided to remove that part as well on the previous book. I want to say again that nothing good comes out of the stipulation of agreement because it has been designed by those who committed wrongdoings towards me, in order to continue to commit wrongdoings towards me in the future. The stipulation of agreement was designed by those who do not want to admit that they were wrong and accused me wrongfully on purpose to get me fired. I was forced to accept the stipulation of agreement despite of all problems and contradiction that contained in it. I had been told to agree and signed it if I want to go back to work. Therefore, I had no choice. At the very end of the stipulation of agreement stated that the case closed with prejudice.

I knew for fact that those who fired me were up to something. The account manager, the one who fired had this smile in his face which make me uncomfortable, and looked at what happened to me as a joke. That was strange of the account manager trying to pin all of the problems and all of the guilt on me by saying that I started with a clean slate and everything was forgiving. In order words, the account manager and the others still did not admit that they were wrong and fire me wrongfully on purpose. They sent me to work to a new place that was worse than the one I was fired from. One the fifth day at the place, they started to make ridiculous cases against me which back fire on everyone involved, particularly the account manager. They tried to be clever (sneaky, slicky, and sleazy) about trying to use one part of the stipulation of agreement against me. I wonder how they would do without having strong and concrete evidence against me. Therefore, I did all of the work to save myself from the problems and lies they created. The workload was on my hand, along with the ability and capability to save myself from the problems and lies. I did all of the work to bring all of the issues that the workplace suffered from to the Vice President who hired me and the gentleman from the Union. I also report about the problems that I was accused of wrongfully on purpose and unfairly. Few months later, I decided to ask for a permanent spot when I kept being accused wrongfully on purpose and unfairly, if the company did not want me to report everything to Authority.

The worse thing that one of them did to me was to get angry at me and threaten to call police on me when I found out that they sent me to work to a place that did not exist. I told them to come to show the place after I spent an hour and half looking for it. The person even added that why did not I quit. Therefore, it was evident that everything that they did to me was done on purpose so that I could quit. I spent more of my time on bench and lost nearly fifteen hours almost per week in nearly five months. It was very wrong for someone like that tried to call police on me while I was waiting for my paystub, after they did what they did to send me home without pay for the day. Why should I be held responsible and accountable for the mess that these people created? However one out among the others witnessed behind closed door saw that I was fired under injustice which done so under power and privilege, without having strong case against me. The real reason why I was fired by the account manager of the site was that he tried to protect his buddies, who happened to be site supervisors and field supervisors. The account manager knew about all the offense, injustice, and wrongdoing the first supervisor had committed for years not only towards some of the employees of the company, but also towards non-employees of the company. Someone who used to make delivery in the building told me one day that be careful with this guy because he is a trouble maker. I heard from few people told me that the company never did anything about the problems. The reason why that happened was that no one even did effective work to expose all of the wrongdoings. On the day I was fired, the account manager of the site told me I was fired because the company did not do details at what happened and I caused so much damage. However, I was not the one who drew the first blood, when the first supervisor was unable to do his job in time of hardship, but effectively threw employees he supervised under the bus to save himself. Everyone in the company, including the account manager and his boys knew what I am capable of doing, and knowing that I was the last person in the company to deal with at creating problems. I began to see that some people are problem makers, producers, and creators. How the problems in this world would fixed or lower to some extent when there are individuals like that everywhere always have the intention to create, produce, and invent problems.

I did not get hired that easily. I have been put into test and I should deliver in any possible ways. They sent me to work in the place I was fired from without knowing that I was into some kind of secret mission. Human resource promised me to go somewhere else and the gentleman who did the first interview told me that things may change when I went to second interview which was the crucial one. The second interview happened by one of the bosses, the vice president and the assistant. The vice president reviewed my resume and found that the resume was heavy. Therefore, I was hired by the vice president, not by the account manager. Otherwise, I would not get hired by the account manager if the account manager was handling the hiring process due to my resume. Therefore, it was disrespectful and shameful of the account manager towards the vice president to fire me under injustice in order to save his buddies. I keep my case prepare and follow the same strategy I have in the previous and current book. I have to do what is necessary to get the people who caused the problem towards me, to get caught into the abyss of their problems and predicaments. I do so without caring about their classes, races, ranks, and backgrounds because they do not matter to me when people ended being irresponsible, careless, arrogant, and ignorant of their actions. The gentleman from the union wondered how I manage to survive the first supervisor for a long period of time when he already knew the type of person the supervisor was. I omitted the word that the gentleman from the union used to describe the supervisor because it was a bad name. I did not give him an answer when he asked me about that at the end of the last meeting. I have a chance to include that on the book. I survived the supervisor because I had respect for him. I was the only one in the workplace that had respect for him than anybody else. His kind does not have respect for him. The supervisor was a kind of person who likes to create enemies. Everyone thought that we were buddies, but we could have been buddies. I could say that he was good at managing the fire command station. I learned from him about that.

There are few events that contributed to my termination under injustice. Those events occurred from end of May to the beginning or middle of September 2016. I doubt that few other events before that were contributed to my termination. These few events were not I to get blame for them, but the person who caused them happened because of his anger and stupidity. That person also went along and committed lies which came back to bite him and few months later accused of something that I did not do, which could prove otherwise on cameras for both events. The first event happened at the end of May 2016 from the arrogant and ignorant employee that I mentioned on the previous book. The employee said that he did bad things to people, as long as he was not the one going to suffer the consequence of his wrongdoings. A person like that said something towards others is for real and there was no joke about that. He did things that could jeopardize my job and others who may not see it. Therefore, I reported to the account manager about them twice. However, he did not listen. One of the problems that I had with him was that he did not relief me properly the way the first supervisor asked him to do. He also did not have respect for the first supervisor. I would not save him from any problem he putted himself into because of his arrogance and ignorance. He should not be the way he was as someone who claimed to have education. I did the best I could to help out on two issues he was in on his first day on the job on Saturday morning. He was lucky that I worked that Saturday because of a special work that went on in one of the clients' space upstairs. I was doing the loading dock. I had to abandon my post which I should not, just to help him out. I understand that he worked security for the first time and did the lobby for the first time all by himself to deal with unexpected events that happened once in a while.

The first event was that he stopped two tenants on his first day on the job that Saturday. The first tenant was a girl who happened to leave her apartment key in her office. She spent nearly two hours or less than that at the lobby and unable to get to her office due to her absence of her access card. I heard him over the radio asking the engineers who were there for the special assignment as well. The engineer said that it not their jobs, but only security. Therefore, I abandoned my post just to help the tenant out. I found out that another tenant came in to help the tenant and unable to find her keys at her desk. I found it kind of strange to some degree there. I went upstairs with the tenant so that she could get her keys. The information about the tenants is at the front desk computer system. I told him to make a log entry in the log book about the matter. Few minutes later, I went to the front desk and hoping that he reported the way things happened accordingly, which was not. The entry should have been a paragraph long, not very few sentences that appeared to be that I did something wrong. I had a feeling I would be questioned by the first supervisor on Monday about it, which turned out to be true. The supervisor tried to find way around it to make it a problem to have me removed from the place, or intend to get me fire. However the supervisor could not because of the response I gave to him about what actually took place that day. The camera would prove everything.

The second tenant came in about one or two hours later. I heard him over the radio again and I abandoned my post to go the front desk. I found out that the tenant turned out to be the CEO of one of the companies upstairs. The tenant told me that he scan his access card at the front door and got in. The tenant added that he was unable to get access through the turnstile with his access card. I found that management of the building may have forgotten to add access for him to be in the building over the weekends. I even checked his name on the computer and found about his information and his picture (which some people think it does not matter if they do have their pictures on the computer for identifications). I gave him access. I told him to go to see management on Monday to request access in the building over the weekends. I added that it was not management's fault, but simply forget to do that. I took the log book and made the entry about that matter. The supervisor saw the second entry and did not question about it when it well written and organized in order. The only thing that he told was not to make entries like that on the log book, which he was wrong about that on purpose because he does not want records of anything like in the log book so that he can find his way around to get people in trouble which could led to termination, write ups, or suspension. Another thing that may appear to be an issue there was a loophole that I found out the policy that happened on the post order. The post order stated that tenants must have their access cards to work on the weekends, otherwise no access would be granted by security officers. I wonder does the same rule apply to a tenant who came to work on the weekends got into building with the access card, and not through the turnstile. The entrance door was the main access. I would not blame any security officers who find themselves into situation like that by following a policy that prove to have problem later one. Therefore, the law in theory is not the same as the law in practice. What I did that day was that to prevent unnecessary and unwanted problem that could have happened, when someone should have been blamed for everything, particularly when that person is innocent of everything. I did not do this for security at the desk but tried to bring peace to the problem and moved on. I also have to take responsibility because I worked at the site before he did. He was under my responsibility indirectly and he was lucky that I was there to do his job for him while I abandoned mine.

Few months later, I discovered that he was arrogant, ignorant, ungrateful, and inconsiderate person. He was on his own to deal with all of the problems that would happened in the future for two reasons. The first reason was that he already passed his probation time which means he should be able to do the work at any level. The second reason base on his arrogance and ignorance, and did things on purpose trying to get me and others in trouble. I sent few letters to the account managers about he did not relief me properly to be at the messenger center before closing hour, and I would not be held responsible and accountable for his mess. One of the major problem that he caused was he failed to make entry in the log book what time that the contractors finished using the freight for the special work that took place in one of the client's floor. That should have had him got fired on the spot not only for not doing his job, but also his arrogance and ignorance that he projected toward the supervisor when the supervisor confronted him about it. The supervisor and I knew that if it was people of color doing what he did, the supervisor would not even waste his time to talk with him or her, but fired that person immediately with his written report that would base on injustice. I was there when the supervisor confronted him and the supervisor tried to hide from the cameras because he does not want his behavior exposed like that. I witnessed what happened and someone who came to do test on the fire command station witnessed everything as well. I simply walked out of the desk and stood about ten feet away from it to do my job. I found it absurd of the supervisor to come to talk to me about the issue and wondered if he forgot who was doing the loading dock that night. However, I should have done the loading dock that night, but the supervisor changed that and had me on the floor where the worked occurred. Management asked the supervisor to go get the accurate time the contractors used the freight so that they can send bill to the contractors for using the freight. That was about a month or month and half later after the worked was done, and management asked the supervisor for the record. I had to remind the supervisor that I was not doing the loading and my position was changed by him.

Around the same April of 2016, one of the security officers was forced to leave his post due to his condition. He was not feeling well but decided to keep on working. He left work at about two or three hours later. However, the office could not find someone on the spot to replace the security officer. The office sent someone to work the remaining one hour. They sent that temporary security officer to post at the messenger center with him. However, I wondered why my position changed that day because I usually the one closed the messenger center on weekdays. The supervisor told me to stay at the loading dock for the day. There was something that happened while I was at the loading dock which was almost costed me my job on the very first day on the site. It was not my fault and another security officer was at the loading did not get involve immediately to help out. That security officer was there before I was and already pass his probation time. He decided not to do anything. I was already got a write up from the supervisor and nearly got me fired or kicked out of the site. It was not a problem, but the supervisor made it a problem so that I could be in trouble. The issue was that some messengers sometimes just dropped packages at the loading by saying that it is for us and walked away. We as security officers at the messenger center do not hold packages for anyone, but sign the messengers in and sent them upstairs until we got approval from the clients. Some messengers also need security escort to go upstairs because it depends on the clients.

I could not stand a new security officer got into trouble for something that he did not know about, and he was under our responsibilities to make sure that some officers should not gotten into any trouble, unless if he or she brought it to himself or herself. I saw the messenger walked toward to get out through the loading dock instead walked out through the lobby. I stopped the messenger and told him that where he was going. He said that he dropped the package at the messenger center. I told him that he had to bring it upstairs. I took a look at the messenger center and found out that the new temporary officer was all alone. I abandoned my post just to find out where the security officer was. The new officer told me that it has been about thirty minutes since the security officer told him that he went to use restroom. The officer did not even let me and the fire safety director at the lobby that he was about to use restroom, and kept an eye out for him. He did not have to tell me about that, but simply made an announcement on the radio about that. I called the client upstairs, to get approval from them to send the messenger upstairs to do the delivery. I went to the log book to make a report about my action and included what the new temporary officer told me about everything just to protect myself and him. When the security officer came back where ever he came from and found out from the new officer about everything, he knew that he was in trouble. The officer tried to make me go to the messenger center as if he gave me an order. I told him that I could not go because the supervisor told me to stay at the loading dock for the day.

He was mad and loud, as soon as he came to work on the next day at the lobby. The lobby is echoes and one could hear anyone talk even though they talk at normal tone of voice. I could hear him accused me of wrongdoing when actually I did not include his name on the entry that I wrote. I wonder how the situation would have been if I did not get involve, but simply did what the other security officer who was there before I did. I was under suspicious that the supervisor would use the opposite of the issue against me. The supervisor could have said that I had enough change to get involve to help out but I did not. What about the same issue that I was in? I was doing the messenger center all by myself at the end of the shift. I wonder if the supervisor talked with the security officer at the loading dock about the issue. The supervisor even showed me a snap picture from the camera at the loading dock that the security officer at the loading dock saw the messenger walked passed him and he did not stopped the messenger. I simply told the supervisor that the messenger told me that the package was for us instead of saying that the package was for one of the clients. I ended up delivered the package to the client. The client happened to be the one who reported the issue that seemed not to be an issue to the supervisor. I did not know who at the office told the supervisor to let something that seemed not to be an issue to go away. The supervisor had enough opportunity to have him fired or removed from the site base on what the security officer did that day. The security officer seemed to do what he did on purpose so that the new temporary security officer could have getting blame for something that was not his fault or problem.

One day of May 2016, on Wednesday the supervisor asked me if I wanted to work on Sunday because of a special work that should take place at the loading. The type of work was that to be there at four o'clock until completion. It did not matter if I did not work the whole shift that was stated on the memo. I could leave as long as what should be taking care of and leave. The office and management of the building knew that I would work that Sunday. The schedule was even in the memo at front desk, loading dock, and messenger center. However, I worked the morning shift and waited for a relief to be at the loading dock. The security officer happened to be my relief that Sunday. He came close to be late and relief me from the front desk nearly ten minutes after four pm. When he came in before relief me, he has a slur remark about the locker room key that was not at the front desk. He knew who had the key and it was absurd of him to criticize me about my professionalism. I did not know what my professionalism had to do about the locker room key. The security officer I relief that morning sometimes went home with the lock room key by mistake. That happened many times. I did not say anything at all when he said that he did not know why I did security. It was the security officer who was at the loading dock on the first day I worked on the site which did not do anything about the messenger issue who went home with the locker room key. I wrote down the time I was not at the front desk. It seemed to be that he did not appreciate that I wrote down the time he relief me at the front desk exactly. I just simply followed protocol which he knew about. I decided to go out quick to buy some food. I did so while the porter was around for more than seven hours to do some special cleaning in and out of the building. Otherwise, I would stay in the building until the work completed. When I came back and went to the messenger center to eat while I kept my eyes on the monitor. As soon as I done I went to the lobby to make sure that no one used the lobby to bring anything heavy at the lobby. The security officer stopped me and told me that I should not be here and he called the office to report about that. I told him that I was and check the payroll. I tried to save him from the problem that he created on purpose. He was so mad and loud until the porter heard noises from the freight while he was on his way out. The porter decided to come to the lobby to see what was going on. The security officer told me with anger that he was not playing with me, and he would show me to show him respect. He said that to me before the porter came to the lobby. I found it absurd of someone asked me to show him respect when I did not disrespected him on the first place. The security officer was determined to kick me out in front of the porter. He did not want me to do entry in the log book while I took the log book away to be at the messenger center to do an entry about his behavior and I would not be held responsible for his behavior. I decided to go to the locker room and change. One of the field supervisors was there and told me that where I was going. I told the supervisor that the security officer made the called to leave the place and I would leave. The field supervisor told me that I was not going anywhere. I went down to change back. I went back to the lobby and the field supervisor told me something that he should not have to about why I listen to the security officer. I told the supervisor that the company better stopped hiring (the four words I used omitted) people like him to work for the company. The field supervisor asked the security officer to apologize to me which I rejected his apology because the security officer done what he did on purpose. The work that should have had done at the loading dock, happened at the lobby while the conversation took place. I told the field supervisor that the security officer would be held responsible and accountable for the work now. I told the field supervisor about few of the major offenses that the security officer committed I knew of in the past. The field supervisor said to me that the site supervisor never reported to the office about those major offenses. The field supervisor told me that to stay at the loading to work all of the hours stated on the memo. I worked the whole hours and had enough time to do another entry on the log book, which turned out to be serious problem for the security officer. I made an incident report on top of that on the next and send it to the account manager.

The account manager came to the site either on the next or on Tuesday and talked to me about what happened. The account manager told me that the security officer told him that I called him bastard. The word bastard was not among the words I told him, and the field supervisor knew and witnessed the words I used but indirectly to the security officer. I told the account manager that said I that. I added that the account manager should go back to the security officer and asked if I said that before or after the situation happened. I never got any response from the account manager, but told me that he would be removed from the place over the phone. I also took responsibility for the word in case if the issue became serious in the future. I also do so that I could get the security officer more in trouble and dragged everyone along with him on the trouble. The account manager knew what type of person that the security officer was and wondered why the security officer last longs enough on the workplace. I was under suspicious that there must have been some kind of favoritism going on which I could care less about. That favoritism would use against those who made it happened to begin with. The security officer never reported what actually happened, along with the slur remark. Therefore, it was the two incident reports I wrote led to his termination. I would not know what was going to happen if did not do anything at all.

The last issues that happened later on had to do about the supervisor. There were few issues that happened on August 2016 which they could have been taking care of, instead of looking for scapegoats (or patsies) to blame all on. The first issue was two security officers told me that the supervisor cursed them over the phone which was unnecessary and unwanted on June or July 2016 of the supervisor. The first one, a Caucasian male, told me that the supervisor called the workplace about something and cursed him over the phone about it when I came that morning. I remembered someone called out and the office wanted someone to come a little bit early to fill the empty spot. I called the office and told them they should have had called and I would showed up. The supervisor knew that as well, and I wondered why he did otherwise. The supervisor knew that he could not talk to me in certain ways that could get him in trouble. The supervisor would not give me the opportunity to make cases against him. The new girl, a young Latina, who just got hire and nearly to be done with her probation time told me the same thing, when she came to work the same morning. She was mad about the way the supervisor talked to her over the phone. The girl would show up to work anyway and the supervisor should not have cursed her over the phone. The new girl must have reported that at the office but the office seemed to never do anything about that. There was a saying in my country said that "rotten teeth has power or force on sweet plantains." That means that some people have power or force on the weak. Therefore, that was what happened there.

The second issue could not be specified on the book, but only by reading between the lines. Another new girl came to the site. She had been working with the company for few years but the office decided to put her where I worked. She happened to replace the security officer who was fired after his nonsense and stupidity. It was not anyone's fault about what happened that day on the afternoon which affected all of us, which almost led to all the security officers' termination from the workplace. What happened that day, happened to one of the places I used to work for my previous employer? The place was secured and there were building security officers at the lobby and security officers work for the clients. Nobody gets blamed for the problem because of technological issue which may appear as a glitch. The same thing happened that day where I worked. I saw the footage of the issue and the new girl who got suspended for a day which she did not care about the suspension was on guard. The supervisor was mad at her. I decided to take matters into my hand when I found out that the field supervisor and the supervisor were buddies and they dumped the responsibility on the female security officer. The major issue there was that the supervisor used the camera from above to draw ridiculous conclusion on the issue. I do not have to see what he wrote but knowing for sure that was what he used to put on his report. There was a problem there because looking at something from above is not the same way looking at it at the bottom. There was a technological issue which seemed to be ignored by the supervisor. I did not mean to go above anyone just to prove anything, but simply tried to save the others and I of an issue which was unable to handle by the supervisor and the field supervisor appropriately, properly, and effectively. I delivered one to management of the building and one to the office to the account manager. I do not know what happened later on with that until later on it came back to me when I had to deal with the vice president who hired me over everything that happened that month. The female officer was innocent of what happened. What happened that day could have had happened to anyone regardless their levels of smartness and ranks.

The third issue had to do about that one of the clients accused security about letting unauthorized visitors on their floor. It was an honest mistake and who knew if some of the employees of the company done so and no one suspected anything. However, the client should partially gotten blame for the problem as well. Two of the employees from the company came down stairs and accused security about giving access to unauthorized visitors. I was the only one there at the desk. That happened around two or close to three o'clock on the afternoon. These two employees went on to report about that to management. However what happened which caused the problem was that there was a group of people that came in and told us that that they had an appointment they would come back later. Another group came about ten minutes later told us that they had an appointment. The security officer who was in the front with me had been a senior for ten years or more in the building and I checked the visitors to see if they had been pre-registered. If they not, we called the client to let them know about their guess or visitors are in the building and they are not pre-registered. The first group that was there somehow came in and mixed with the second which turned out that half of them had not been pre-registered. We even asked them if they were the same group which nobody answered. We tried to call the client which there was no host phone number available to call in case any anomalies happened. Therefore, we just assumed that everyone know each other and sent them upstairs. It was not the first time that security had to deal with issue that groups of people are dispersed at the lobby. It made our work hard to figure out who is who and where they need to go before we send anyone to the wrong floor by mistake which might turn out to be big problem for us.

I came early on the next day and started to write an incident report about the issue. I spoke to the supervisor about it as soon as I came in. The supervisor was the one who told me it was too late and everything already bought to management upstairs. Later on the afternoon, the seniority security officer and I had been interrogated individually about the issue by a new field supervisor. The supervisor in the meantime was looking for ways to make matters worse, so that both of us could either loss our job, or removed from the place with suspension. I was the last one that the field supervisor interrogated about the issue. I told them that the very beginning of the issue had been ignored by the supervisor because I told him the time that the first group came in and checked what happened. I told the field supervisor that I came this morning to write a report about what happened and the supervisor said it was late to do so. I told the field supervisor that we checked everyone and found out that there was no phone number of the host available for those who were not pre- registered, in case of trying to call the host. I wondered how this situation would have had handled if we were not blacks or African Americans. I do not blame the other security officers particularly the senior officer who everything that had been going on that month frustrating him out. Who wants to be frustrated to higher level? We found that month happened to be the month that some issues happened frequently as if there was some kind of dark force which made them happened.

The fourth issue was all on the supervisor. He used to tell me that he has the easiest job. The job of not doing anything, gotten pays more than us, and dumped his responsibility on us which we have been labeled as "subordinate". I do not like the meaning that came along with the word. It is a word that associated with **slavery**. I did him a favor to get the list of people who did not have pictures for their access cards. I did so after the supervisor told me that the lady I stopped for that problem reported to him that I was harsh on her which was not true. The tenant ignored me by saying that she did not have time for that. Otherwise, the supervisor may have made things up by saying other than what may have reported to him. Above all, this is childish from some people who continued think that they are better than anyone who are at the bottom of them. The big issue is that some people may have two different last names. The information on their access cards have one full name, and it is a different issue when they try to get a temporary pass for the day by given security a different full name. The issue that I had to deal with that day happened on the place I went to work for my previous employer just for training. The lady gave me her name and I could not find the last name that she gave me to give her a temporary passes. She gave me another last name few minutes later and found her in the system. This problem could have been avoided if the person and everyone remember the name that they use to do something. I do not think people would go to their banks and mistakenly give different first or last names, or wrong banking account to take care of their business. Otherwise, that appears as security breach on their banking account even though they make honest mistake. Therefore, it is their responsibility to remember what they did to have something and to remember everything about it. That is the kind of world that we live because most of us who are at the bottom of society have so much going on. Who know how many of us have more than ten usernames and passwords for different accounts to deal with on our daily lives, while we have so much more to deal with in our lives. Therefore most of us suffered from responsibility effects and issues in modern society. There are things in life that required me to have usernames and passwords that I try to avoid of having them on the first place, unless if I have been forced by the authorities to make my life depends on it. I try to avoid them because I do not have time to remember the usernames and passwords for them, as well as hackers might get access on your sensitive information on your account and ended stealing your identity. One of the accounts that I used to have and I decided to let it go is my Facebook account. I opened my Facebook account because of one personal thing I wanted to do and it turned out unsuccessful. My Facebook account turned out to be blocked because I forget what I putted at the end of my password. I have been told by the company that my account had been compromised; I need to open a new account with a new email address and a new password. Therefore, that proved that the system is vulnerable and unsustainable. I could have use a new password instead of using a new email address and a new password. It has been a decade or since I have a Facebook account.

Let's go back to the issue of what happened that day. It was one Wednesday morning about the hour of ten in the morning that the girl whom the supervisor cursed over the phone was at the front desk with me to further her training. This tenant, a female, Caucasian, around her mid-sixties went out without her access card. She came back and told me that she left her access card at her office. I asked her for her last name. However I could not find her on the system. I called the supervisor on the radio to tell him the front desk needed him quick and there was an issue that required his attention. I did not remember what was his answer was but he did not want to come down to the lobby. I called over the radio to tell him that he needed to come down right now while everyone on the radio listened to my voice (management, security, and engineers). The girl was there witnessed everything and helped out as well and unable to get the tenant's information. The tenant was frustrating about everything because she spent almost ten minutes and unable to go up to her office. I did the best I could to tell her that what happened was not her fault. The supervisor came down stair and checked out all of the moves that we made and asked the lady if she had another last name. The lady responded yes and gave the other last name. The lady had another last name and failed to give it to us and how security should have known about something like that. I found out that this problem had been there about three to four years before I started to work for the company. The supervisor tried to be clever by calling the lady on the other side, took a picture of her and called receptionist where the lady work to make the changes. The supervisor at the end used the camera to appear that I did not do my job and he came down to do my job for me. I knew where this is going. I took the previous record by printing the pass out and had the current record as well. I did so before the previous record went out of existence in few hours later. You all should know what that mean. Anyone could not get prosecuted if the evidence had been disappeared. I told the supervisor that when I called you to come down, you come down. The supervisor sent me to ten minutes break and wondered why he did such thing. However, he was up to something. I did the best I could with those ten minutes to write incident report of what happened.

The supervisor's buddy, the field supervisor, came in. It seemed to be that field supervisor happened to be the one they sent on the site when a situation escalated. I was upstairs I showed him about what happened. The field supervisor told me that he was confused about everything. I told the supervisor that I started to write an incident report about what happened. He said great, but I knew that the bastard did not mean it. It was about thirty minutes later the field supervisor called me on my phone twice to force me out to go to see the vice president, and wondered why. I did the best I could to finish the incident report at the time of pressure, hardship, and bullying. Therefore, bullying is the oldest form of racism (I learned that from a TV series recently while I produce the book). I mentioned in the previous book about that one has to be prepared for the unexpected and the impossible. That was what happened here, I did not know what lay ahead but I will find out when I get there due to the matter of time. I went to the office and faced the vice president who hired me. The vice president told me that what I did would get a lot of people fire and wondered who. The vice president even told me that I should take responsibility. The vice president was not been clear and specific about how I should take responsibility. I do not want any innocent people got fired for what I did. One of the issues that happened previously somehow came back to me. The issue was the one that had to do about the failure of technology. The vice president told me that I should not do such thing by reporting to management about what happened. However, the vice president did not tell me that I sent the same thing to the office. What I did was to do the best I could to save the others and I of something that was not our fault and mistake. The vice president even told me that the other issue had been taking care of and wondered how it had been taking care of. The other issue was the one that security had been accused by the client of having unauthorized visitors to their floor. All I could think of was that I was going to get fire again for no reason. I began to get relief a little to the point when the vice president told me about one of the issue had been taking care of. The vice president even told me that the supervisor was at a meeting. That was the first lie. The supervisor was not in any meeting. The supervisor always told us that when he went to a meeting. The only meeting that we know happened once a week every Tuesday which usually took place at the management office at the penthouse. The supervisor had to come with evidence of that meeting, unless if it was a personal meeting that he had to take care of his personal thing that no one knew anything about. I offered the vice president my incident report. The vice president took a look at by skimming to it, particularly at the end of it. The vice president told me that gave the incident report to the vice president. I began to find out that the supervisor made a second attempt to get me remove from the site or got me fired. The supervisor wrote a report about me and accused me of trying to ruin the reputation of the company. I do not see what reputation of the company that I ruin other than I asked him to do his job. Otherwise, the supervisor used the company as an excuse and advantage to hide all of his mess behind it. The vice president told me something was going to happen before I left, but I could not be specific by that without the vice president consent on that. Therefore, I knew what must be done, but wait for things to happen at their natural course. I did know man like the supervisor already. People like him always want to stir some problem and trouble. The vice president told me that I could not go back to work for the day due to the stage I was in. I told her that I am fine I could go back to work. I went to the workplace and gave the supervisor the incident report and told him that the vice president told me to give that to him. I found it absurd of the supervisor to tell me that if I had problem with him while he walked out of the messenger's office. I responded no, even though that "no" means "yes".

One morning about a week later from that incident, I was at the messenger center on my way back to the lobby. The girl whom the supervisor cursed over the phone was there along with a new girl who was there for training. One of the tenants came in through the loading dock and found his way to the lobby with this look on his face. Those type of look that some people giving when something is not right. I know that tenant because he and other few tenants sometimes came to the messenger center to say hello to us and the lobby as well. The lobby usually gets that because that is where everyone comes in and out of the building. As I walked to get to the messenger center, I saw the security officer sat calmly and tapped one of her feet on the ground gently as if she tried to control her emotion and anger. I also saw little tears came out of her eyes as if blood has been spilled. I could not get any specification out of what happened, but I heard the supervisor said that the tenants are not your friends. I got a sense that the security officer may have said something that appeared as slur remark to the supervisor. The supervisor used that as an advantage to get her removed from the place. Otherwise, the security officer may have used the slur remark as a way to disrespect the supervisor for cursing her over the phone and the office never did anything about that and allowed the supervisor to get away with it. One the next day the usual field supervisor came to the site so that the security officer should get her belonging out of the place. I saw the field supervisor and the site supervisor talking at the corner of the messenger center suspiciously. Therefore, I knew something was up and wrong, I decided to get involve on the situation. I wrote a report to send it to the vice president about not what happened with the security officer, but also other issues as well. I did the best I could to salvage what I found out to write report. I include all of the security officers who had been hurt on the report regardless their races. I want the supervisor to get taste of his own medicine by trying to be clever. I used the past of what the supervisor did against the supervisor. What I did was not based on revenge, but based on days of reckoning. I delivered the report at the office to give to the vice president. On the next day I was on break and I heard that the office called me and I should call back. The office had my cellphone number and they did not call me on it. I called back and no one answered. I went to the office the same day to take care of some private matter and no one approached me and told me they needed me for the report. At the end of August, another field supervisor came in to replace the supervisor as another supervisor. The new supervisor used to be a field supervisor. He used to come to the workplace. It was like moving from one bastard to another which was done under favoritism. Some people did not know that the first supervisor got fire. The one that replaced him only had eight hours of training which was not enough to know about everything in the building. Therefore, they dumped the new supervisor under our responsibilities. The new supervisor began to mess things up on purpose because he gave everyone else hard time, particularly me for no reason at all. I want to say something before I go further. The first supervisor did something on purpose. The supervisor shorted me eight hours. I went to the office to find out if the office made mistake or not. The dispatcher I spoke about with told me that it was the supervisor who shorted me eight hours in one of the day. I went to the site to talk to him about that in front of the new supervisor. The supervisor got the guts and nerve to tell me how I know about which day I did not get pay for. I responded to him by saying that dispatcher told me about it and he had done it on purpose.

As few weeks past and those few weeks was hell for us. I do not blame the others if they felt angry and frustrated that nothing changes at all. One day the new supervisor did something and I asked him was he trying to make my life a living hell. The new supervisor responded yes that was what he doing to me. I said thank you and I walked away. The new supervisor even accused me of saying that I had been disrespectful toward the account manager. These are the types of people that we have to deal with in this life continue to accuse people wrongfully on purpose because they cannot find ways to get me in trouble. I sent a report and the last one to the account manager explaining to him about that we are not going to be held responsible and accountable for the new supervisor's mess. I let the account manager knew that he done things on purpose to make my life a living hell. One Saturday afternoon, the account manager called me on my phone. He told me that he changed my schedule for next week due to the construction that occurred in one of the floors. He changed my schedule because the security officer who had been doing the fire watches was on vacation. He told me it was an option when I knew it was an obligation so that he wanted the new supervisor to be fully in charge while I would not be at the lobby. The account manager knew that he changed my schedule for that purpose, not on my skills. I said no problem. No account manager ever called me on the weekends to change my schedule before. One the first day before I began to work, the office, referred to dispatch sent someone to do the fire watch. The new supervisor told him that to go back to the office. As I began to do the work and found out that I have been exploited because there was about three type of construction occurred on the floor. One of them was nearly done. The other two just started. I found out that there should have been at least two fire guards to do the work. The security officer who did the construction had been exploited despite as Caucasian in his mid-seventies. I have to spend the whole shift from Monday to Friday walking around to check on things.

It is not my problem that the account manager and the new supervisor did not take care of the problem that surrounded the schedule. I have been working the shift that they provided me with and I stick with it. On Thursday, there was an entrapment at the freight elevator. I heard from one the security officer, seniority, told me that the new supervisor called the elevator company and never reported about the entrapment. The security officer told me that he was busy taking care of the visitors and later aware that the elevator company had not shown up in almost an hour and a half. The security officer called the elevator company to find out about if there was a delay. The security office found out from the elevator company that they received a phone call, but whoever called before never reported about the entrapment. The new chief building manager was angry at the new supervisor about that. Before I left on Friday and tried not to work the schedule on the following week due to the issue of the schedule. I was there for the fire watch, not for something else when actually the work I was there for was done for the day. I checked everywhere before I left that Friday to make sure all of the contractors were gone. One contractor came in and told me that he would do some work for few hours all of the sudden. That work had nothing to do with fire work. I decided to leave since it was not my problem because I do not know anything about other work that happened on the afternoon. It was the account manager and the new supervisor responsibility. I told them already that I would not work the shift on the next following week. There was a witness that Friday before I left work. The witness was the chief engineer of the building saw me walked around at the end of the shift to make sure that everything was fine. The new supervisor was at the lobby to come upstairs about the situation. The new supervisor found out about the situation and asked me if I wanted to stay for extra few hours. I told the supervisor I won't be able to do so because I had things to do after work. I did stayed working extra hours for two days already which seemed they did not take that into account and consideration.

I was out on Monday and went to take the FSD test which I took before from my previous employer and got screwed over once when it comes to the onsite test. I got screwed over again. I found shocked that both times I got screwed over resulted to unfair termination twice by the account managers. I will give details about the first time that happened later on. I came to work on Tuesday and the first thing that the new supervisor told me that he reported to the account manager about what happened last week Friday. I do not know what happened last week Friday, but knew for sure that the new supervisor reported lies to the account manager. The account manager and everyone involved knew that the supervisor reported lies to them. Everyone at the office knew what type of person that I am and I would not put myself into any kind of stupid situation that could get me fired, as well as I am a black individual. I did not say anything at all, but waiting to see what would come next. The account manager came to the workplace on the afternoon. The account manager was not being clear and specific about what had been reported to him. I told the account manager that I came this morning and I heard from the supervisor about the report. I told the account manager that I will send my report as well later to him by email. The account manager gave me his business card. The account manager did not want me to send anything to him, but simply wanted me to tell him about what happened verbally. A situation like that does not require me to keep things verbally when the bastards who committed the problem kept things in written. It was like they have the power, right, and privilege to do so, but I am not. I faced the reversal type of the old racism there. The old type that the blacks were illiterate and unable to learn to keep the blacks down and accused the blacks for a problem they did not commit.

It was a surprise for the account manager when I sent response to them in a form of incident report sheet, which was very serious for him and the new supervisor. I came to work on the next day (Wednesday) and delivered the original report to the new supervisor. The supervisor came to me few minutes later and told if that was the way I wanted to go. I did not say anything at all. There was a lady who did not have picture for her access card and I stopped her to take her picture. The new supervisor got involved and told her that not to worry about that she could go because he was the supervisor. That was effectively that the new supervisor slapped his title on my face. It would be under the new supervisor's responsibility to deal with that issue because he knew that he was wrong to let the lady left without taking her picture for her access card. I made an entry in the log book as a record that the new supervisor would be held responsible and accountable for his action. The usual field supervisor showed up at the site and told me to go the office, and wondered why. I was escorted with the field supervisor to the office. I saw something that I was glad that I witnessed it. I saw the field supervisor and the account manager gave each other fist bump and laugh. Therefore, I was fired under injustice. These are the reasons why the account manager told me later on behind a close door that I was fired because I caused so much damage and I should not details about anything that was going on. I went back to the site just get the rest of my belongings the same day. I told the field supervisor who escorted back to the place that storm is coming. The field supervisor thought I meant that physically. I got the rest of my belonging and I told the two of the seniorities who worked at the place that storm is coming while I left the place. I kept walking and I heard someone was laughing out loud outside the loading said good luck. It was the field supervisor who was laughing.

The problems and issues that I had been through with the people at work are examples of that are how the system of the country always has been and needs to be changed. It is the system that gives them all the right, power, and privilege to mess things up and never held responsible and accountable for anything. Therefore irresponsible behavior is truly breeds irresponsible behavior. The problems that I had to deal with from the current and previous employers give me the reality of that is what people of colors has to go through in the world, particularly my home country. I truly found out that when some people catch cold the rest catches pneumonia. It was the one who caused the cold should be held responsible and accountable for creating the problem which led to pneumonia. They ended up blamed their victims with it since they can get away with the mess they created. Who wants to be in relation with someone like that? Some people impose the problems on others and say to those who suffer from the problems to get themselves out of the mess all by themselves. Therefore, firing me under injustice and spent three months without an income was suffering from pneumonia, while suffering from homelessness on top of that.

There was one issue out of the other issues that I found it unfair and the account manager must have been in serious problem with it if there was a trial held in court, on the first meeting. I warned the gentleman from the union that the meeting is useless, worthless, and waste of my time. I also warned the gentleman from the union that if I found any wrong and stupid cases against me, it would be worse for the company. I found out more than four stupid cases against me. One out of the others that I remembered was on that Friday, which led to my termination. The new supervisor knew that there was no problem at all. The account manager and the new supervisor should be held responsible and accountable for the schedule. The lame and stupid case that they had against me was that they tried to make something that was not my business and alienated from as my problem. That was absolutely absurd. I had a speculation about their absurdities. It seemed to be that the account manager and new supervisor were robbing the company and they used me as their personal slave to do all of the work because they took my abilities and capabilities for granted. They both had been exploited the regular fire guard, Caucasian male, and probably his mid-seventies would retire the same year, to do the work. He went on vacation and they passed his shift to me on purpose instead of somebody else. I said before that there should have been at least two fire guards for the work, not one fire guard. The worse thing that happened was the vice president walked out of both meetings when the vice president found that the bastards who fired me had nothing against me, but made fool out of themselves. The account manager even said that he had evidence and he would come with the evidence on the second meeting. However, the account manager did not show up at all on the second meeting, but only the gentleman who served as an attorney was there all by himself. The gentleman from the union told me that the new supervisor would get blamed for everything, and they would go after the new supervisor. It was absurd of the account manager and the others to fire me over lies that they knew about.

I saw the account manager while the elevator landed on the ground level waiting to come in. The account manager saw me and quickly looked down on his phone pretending that he did not see me. I had to go after the supervisor who committed the problem on purpose when I came back to work on January 2017 and ended up spending five days on the place. I did not like the place anyway because it fills with people who have bad and nasty attitude regardless their classes and races. The nasty attitudes come from some of the tenants and crews who work for the building. They sent me to work in the place for punishment. Therefore, the punishment had been used against them which led to the termination of the site supervisor and the loss of contract for the account manager. I went against the issue of what happened that day and over other issues about the place had been disorganized and out of order wondering if they happened on purpose or the account manager and the site supervisor was the one to blame the way they do things on the site. One of the cases that I had against them was that I ended up doing the job for people who had their own people to do it for them. I found it absurd of the site supervisor to tell me to stay in one spot while abandoned it to do somebody else's job. The site supervisor used that against me to get remove from the place. The site supervisor ended up using his supervisory title on me at the same time. The account manager did not want me to send anything to him in writing by email because he would be unable to handle what would come to him.

The vice president who hired me and a gentleman from HR was there on the meeting. The vice president told me that why I accepted the stipulation of agreement when the vice president, the gentleman at the union knew the answer to that question; and I did not respond to that question. Otherwise, going to court with it would effectively backfire on everyone. Despite everything that happened, I just simply did not want to go to court and to authority I usually send my cases to. I do not care about this people's money or lawsuit. I wanted the problem to handle by identifies the threat and eliminate the threat. I only needed to get pay for the hours that I missed for three months that had been fire under injustice which I never get. I also did the best I could to find another job while I was fired under injustice and not succeeded at it from one reason. The reason was security jobs are now downsizing. Some employers now interrogating applicants during the interview to find out the true reason why the applicants wanted to work for them and the reason why the applicants got fired or quit their previous jobs. It is now gotten complicated when employers are now asking applicants' letters of references. It seems to be that letter of references become a new thing almost in all jobs now, particularly the civil service exam positions and College Graduates. The letter of references seems to be a problem because it only apply to those who looking for to survive. I wonder who came up with such thing and why. It is effectively wrong that employers on both public and private asking college graduate such things. Despite that some people have letter of references, that does not mean that they would get the jobs, even though they have all the other qualifications to get the jobs. Despite all, some people would always get opportunities without them even though they would mess things up in the future. Those opportunities would happen under favoritism, not worth deserve.

The reasons why I went against my previous employer was that they did not handle my case properly when it was the new people who took over created all of the problems. They tried to write me up for insubordination to which they did not have any proof about. The new account manager who took over and the others left mess behind when they changed my schedule for one day. They did not know that changed my schedule was a big problem when it was unnecessary for them to do so. Otherwise, they were up to something. They changed my schedule and made a promise which they broke their promise twice. I usually did they patrol of the clients floors at night and did so for nearly two years and half. I ended up working with a lunatic who always caused problem for himself and being a prejudice individual. I was under suspicious that the office changed my schedule to have him worked my shift as punishment. Therefore, the lazy bastard was rebelled about it and dragged me down with him with lies. The bastard called the new account manager about two lies. I was training the guard to work the shift that night and the guard worked the lobby twice before. The bastard called the account manager to report about that he called me for restroom break and I did not give him restroom break. The guard I was training was there and witnessed that the guard at the lobby did not call and asked for restroom break when the new account manager asked the new guard about it. The new guard responded no. Few minutes later, receptionist called me from the intercom to call the lobby desk. I use my phone and putted on speaker and the new guard found it shock that the guard at the lobby reported lies and later on asked for restroom break after.

The second lie was the worse than first lie. I was off duty and I spoke with one of my countryman that worked for the building, and the new guard called me and asked for help. I went to help him out while I was off duty. A gentleman who came in the building earlier while I was at the lobby with the new guard asked for one of the tenants again. I called the tenant and there was no one answers. Therefore, I could not give the gentleman access to go to see the client with approval from the client. The gentleman decided to leave and came back later. I called again and no one answered. It was another tenant who was there told me that the gentleman is fine and he could go upstairs with him. I signed the gentleman in and gave him a pass. The guard came from to his hour break, since it should have had been half hour break, saw everything and decided not to get involve since I did his job anyway. The new account manager called me while I was on my way home. The account manager told me that the guard called him and told him that I gave unauthorized visitor access. I knew where this was going and I told the account manager and the other person involved that I need to keep everything that happened on email, not phone calls. I have been spending a week and a half without work and the ridiculous investigation was not going to work when the account manager knew for fact that I got fire under prejudice, discrimination, injustice, and favoritism. I even asked the new account manager to bring proof of all the allegations that I have against him and the company when he sent me this ridiculous letter by email. I demanded the new account manager that I need to get in contact with his boss so that I would send my case to authority about everything. The new account manager ended up tells me to be at a meeting with management. I warned the new account manager that I would not be good for him and the company if they made me waste my time. Therefore, the meeting was a waste of my time and I was accused by one of the manager that I ended gave them attitude when the new account manager and the other gentleman found out that no attitude came out of me. I had been promised to work to another place and they never called me. Therefore, I decided to bring my case to authority about everything. I had been out of job for a month, while I had to deal with homelessness. I have cases against my previous employer not only under prejudice, discrimination, injustice, favoritism, but also ungrateful and inconsiderate of those who made a mess and they did not want to take full responsibility of their mess. They ended up fire me while I was off duty and double my work that day for no reason at all. They had the intention of write me up for insubordination to which they did not have proof of. Otherwise, the new people who took over looking to get rid of me anyway and they trapped with the guard who caused the problems. They tried to destroy my reputation and had to pay the price of accused me wrongfully on purpose when I did the best I could to help them went after the person who caused the problem. I also lost my job in two days later after I took the FSD exam for the first time.

There were three events that brought the deepest and profound changes in my life. I always say that the year 2008 and 2009 thought me big lessons. The event happened in 2008. I would like to know that how many people in this world would risk or sacrifice their jobs over friends who got themselves in trouble. However, the action I took was not based on risk, but looked at as a chance. I thought it would not be anything, until it appeared otherwise later. There are some people in this world who do not or seem to never learn how to bring control in their life and always want others to help them into something that was their responsibility to begin with. They can do them and wonder if laziness has caused them to be the way they are. I ended up abandoned my work one day of the summer 2007 to go to a friend who asked to use my phone because his phone was not in used. He wanted to call his bank because his phone was disconnected and he did not have money to pay his phone bill. The friend told me that the bank kept taking money out of his direct deposit. He never was being clear and specific why the bank did so. I used to work in a computer lab and I abandoned it to help my friend. I saw the lab office door was locked and my bag pack was locked inside the office.

The supervisor came in shortly and asked me where I was. I told him that I was helping a friend. He told me that I was fired by one of the bosses on the spot for abandoned the lab. The supervisor added that he performed a miracle to get my job back and never do that again. Therefore, I was doing my job on zero chance since that happened. I did not pay attention that my action could have had looked differently from others. Some could have had looked at my action as careless, negligence, irresponsible, and insubordination. I did not aware of the theft activities that happened sometimes on campus. Anyone could have come into the lab and stole computers or monitors while I abandoned the workplace. I would not take the risk if all of these possibilities had been aware before I took action. The friend ended up accused of being a hypocrite when I tried to stay away from the ridiculous friendship because of what he did. I wonder how many hypocrites around the world would risk or sacrifice their anything to save friends who got themselves in trouble. It was a stranger who saved me from my best friend. I just met the stranger on the last day of the cruise I went with him and his brother. The stranger lived in Michigan. The friend gave me her number and we talked. We ended up become a little bit more than strangers, but friends to each other during that few months of talking. Some time we spend nearly an hour talking over the phone. He and I decided to go to Michigan for the first time. I did not want to go with him but he insisted. There are a lot I would omit on the book about what happened there. He decided to blind me from the truth about what he did. I was the sucker to fall for his lies which was very crucial for him to do.

I found it strange that I told him the truth while he told me lies. I also found it strange I saved him while he destroyed me at the same time. That was not a good trade at all in a friendship. He tried to destroy what I had with her. He tried to play both sides and I almost fall for everything because I was consumed by what he said to me about everything. I did something which I could have had ignored what she had to say. I knew for facts that there were things that he did in front of me, her and another person which I did not appreciate at all. I would never let those dump and ridiculous things he did never repeated themselves anymore. There were things that happened that I did not know about even though we were in the same place, but they happened behind closed door. I could not comprehend of the truth of what she told me that my friend did something that I would never expect him to do. The outcome of that action could have had affected me, him, and her. The girl even told me that they blame him for everything and I did not do anything wrong at all. The girl even told me that I should effectively stay away from someone like that permanently. My blood pressure rose to the roof, unable to breathe normally, unable to keep myself up, and tears came out of my eyes as if I had no control to stop it. That was the first time in my life my blood pressure raised that high and I could felt it on my body and through my veins. I did the best I could to sleep that night and unable to finish to speak with her that night. I let her know later on that the friend was more than a friend to me. I never let him suspect anything at all and waiting for an opportunity came along to put an end to that friendship. The friend was a kind of friend who liked to manipulate, play those who appear like a sucker to him. He called me one day and asked me for a favor. I never pick up my phone when I saw his number showed up. He called many times that day left me intimidated messages. I never called him but simply let things stayed the way they were. I went to see the girl two more times after that happened just make up for the mess. The girl just broke down a bad new to me after two years later that she suffered from cancer. She was treated before and though that everything was fine. She did not even want me to come to see her after her operation because she did not look attractive enough for me to see her. I was insisted to come to see her. I thought thing was going to work out and I did not hear from her for two months. She was the oldest in her family. One day my phone rang and found out that her sister called and to give me the news that she passed away about a week ago.

The friend used to tell me about that the other friend was a bad friend without detailing about anything toward the other friend. It had been four years since I saw the other friend. I saw the friend one Friday afternoon of the same week that the earthquake in Haiti occurred. I told the other that I need to speak with him and we should meet in front of the building I lived in on the next day. I was shocked by what the other friend told me. I left all of the details of what the other friend told me out of the book, not only without his consent, but also they are too gruesome to include them. The friend told me that he regretted that he listened to him to do wrong action. The other friend was right. He did try to make me do wrong things and every time he got to that with me, I went after him so strong and powerful. No wonder sometimes he gave me some attitude and slur remarks. I gave him more chance to change his way (more than four chances on major problems), he never did. The other friend even told me that he was in big trouble which he never being clear and specific about them. I just got the most of everything out from other friend than he did. He just simply acted innocent out of everything when he was actually the guilty one. The other friend and I had a suspicious of him being guilty of what he was accused of while in high school. That was how we met and became friend after I heard of the accusation. I felt sorry and sympathized toward what he was accused of. I did not want to draw conclusion on anything, but the other friend drawn absolute conclusion that he was guilty of what he was accused of. I had a chance to get out of the friendship permanently and I took it. I use that experience as a reminder because there are a lot of people with the same mindset like him out there regardless their race and gender. Therefore, I learned from my past to protect my present and future. Therefore, I learn to remember, not to forget.

I have to stay away from people like him before he accused me of being an accessory to a crime he may commit in the future. I do not want to get any phone call from the police told me that I witnessed him of being innocent of a crime he may have accused of. I received a phone call probably from a job that he applied for and gave my name as a reference. The lady left me a voice mail that they running an investigation on him after he applied for the job. I have not spoking with him in two or three years and he used my name without my consent. I decided not to call back and left things the way they are. I found that people like him always want help from others, and they never around to return a small favor. People like him always hurt those who helped them because they are ungrateful, careless, arrogant, ignorant, and disrespectful. People like him tend to be manipulator, narcissist, bully, and player. I knew that he is going to be in big trouble since he did not find me. Everyone that he hurt began to fade away from him completely. He sent me hurtful texting few times and one email in the last past ten years and wonder why. It seems to be that he thought I was a weak and pathetic woman and man who he can come with ridiculous things and hope to be conquered by him so that I could come back to the friendship and suck it up. He thought that I should depend on him when he could not save himself from any problems and issues he faced. That is the problem with dependency. Some people, regardless their genders dump all of their responsibilities to others and expecting them to fix all of their problems instead of them to do otherwise. That is the problems that some people continue to face in the world. They continue to dump their responsibilities to other when others may not able to help at all. I want to say that just we are depending on each, which does not mean we are depending on each other to higher extent. I see some people who have the abilities and capabilities to do a lot of things, but ended up being lazy. Therefore, it is evident that the mind is a terrible thing to waste.

I would be in trouble if I dump all my responsibility to people who could not help me at all, particularly the complex problems that each and every one of us in this world always face. It took me a decade and half to put me where I am and find out that I have to do a lot on massive scale to get a little something out of the system due to the manifesto of racial prejudice. Despite all of the problems and hardship I faced, particularly from those who should have been the one to guide me through things ended up trying to discourage by saying that I would not succeed. One Latina and one male Caucasian in college told me that they faced almost the same thing that I went through when I threw it out there to them. Therefore, I began to use people's negativities and turn them into positivity. I would never go on in this life to discourage anyone regardless their class, race, and gender. I was lucky enough to meet those who give me advice and took what they told me into account and consideration regardless of their classes, races, and genders. I also find out that my responsibility is not only nationally but internationally. The world make it official that we are living in a global economic after the outcome of the world war two. Some people use to say that they start from the scratch. I could say that I was far away from the scratch, trying to get on the scratch, and move away from the scratch. I begin to do the fair share of my responsibilities on both national and international. A friend would never come around to reproach me of something that he knew for facts that he never done, and unable to do the same for himself. I should be the one to do or say that when actually

I never do. I did things for people because that is the way I am. I found it unfair to get something like this from someone who claimed that I was his good and best friend. I also blamed myself even though I was innocent of all the wrongdoings. I blamed myself to make sure that these problems never repeat themselves anymore.

The second event was about a place I worked part time while I started to go to college. It was in the middle of May 2006; I got hired, and ended up working in a museum for the first. That museum used to locate next to MOMA in Manhattan. I see the world come into the museum and most of the arts were great. The chief supervisor was the first and last supervisor that I worked with, who turned out to be fair and just. He was the FSD of the museum as well. He was born in Jamaica. He had the passion to know about the subject of President John F. Kennedy. He read probably most or some of the books related to President John F. Kennedy's subject. He could have been a professor at the university teaching courses on President John F. Kennedy's subject either in Political Science or Sociology. I worked in the museum on the weekends and fill in sometime on the weekdays while off from school, for four years. I messed up because I let someone dragged me into it and did not pay attention that was what the person was looking to make case against me to get me fired or removed from the museum. It was one of the guards who just turned into supervisor. He became supervisor because he replaced the supervisor who left the company. He used to say that he knew how to get people in trouble. He never said that he just provoked people and reported false accusation. He even said that he did not like people tell him what to do, which he meant that he would do other than what the chief supervisor asked him to do.

One Friday night, about seven minutes before making the announcement on the fourth floor that the museum would close. I was just lean my arms on the concrete that was about three to four feet away from the stairs on the middle of the floor which also led down to the third floor. He came to the floor and knew for fact that I was not sleeping, but accused me wrongfully on purpose to get me in trouble. I told him that I was not sleeping. He replied by saying that I should not test his intelligence. I replied again with a control anger by saying I was not f****** sleeping ok. He replied thank you very much. I already knew that I was in trouble. I decided to learn from that mistake and never let it happened anymore.

The chief supervisor was mad about that but wanted to help me by giving my case to him. The chief supervisor did not want to lose me from the museum, but decide to vouch for me and had me send to another place instead of being fired. I told the chief supervisor later what the supervisor told me which caused me angry. The chief supervisor later on told him what I reported and he got caught on that, but too late for me to come back. The chief supervisor even showed me the report the supervisor wrote which full of lies. The supervisor reported what did not take place that day. The camera that used to be on floor had been removed for nearly a year, which could have shown evidence of the incident. I decided to sign the incident report and denied everything that it contained as false. The museum closed down two years later after the incident. The reason why the supervisor did what he did because a year before he messed up into a situation that was his job for them to fix very easily. The supervisor wanted me to abandon my post to do something that I should not. I was doing the lobby which was the main entrance of the museum. I called him about the situation and putted him on speaker. He decided to hang-up on me while few others witnessed it. I spoke with the chief supervisor about that and found out that I was doing my job and I was not responsible for what happened that day. I did not know how the chief supervisor talked to him about the issue, when I told the chief supervisor that to be careful on how he would approach the supervisor. We spend about six to seven months that we never say a word to each other until he came up to me one day talked to me about the presidential debates. We still not talked the way we did before, after the incident took place. The supervisor did what he did just to get even of what happened previously. There were others who were shocked that I was not in the museum anymore and suspected that the supervisor was the cause of it. I also felt so bad about that because I affected the chief supervisor with it, even though it was not meant to happen.

I have been sent to a worse place. I have been sent to works not so far away from John Jay College. I worked in place that has about four condos. The fire works on Fourth of July used to take place there every year and stop. I heard that the company was going under transition, taking over by another company. I worked all summer on that place and decided to change my schedule to work only on the weekend due to school. I used to work on the afternoon and I did not like the afternoon shift. I decided to stick up with it. The chief supervisor and the some of the supervisors who were there while I made the change of my schedule did not like it. It was like as if they did not want to hear the word school at all. There were few events that took place and one of them was totally unfair to remove me from the place and never being call for work. The first event was that one of my country men was wrong at everything. He caused problem for himself and tried to do the same to me. There were about three Haitians used to work at the place. One of them was a supervisor on the morning shift. He left the place a month later because he found a better job. The other one was fine, but never looking to get himself in trouble. The second event was that one of the supervisors wrote me up on purpose over ridiculous lateness. The chief supervisor, the supervisor, and the others knew that I did not have an access card to get into the office in the basement. I came to work one Saturday afternoon and I got into the place at 4pm sharp. My countryman, who was at point (access to park in the garage), saw me coming toward him and knew why, already had his access card out for me to use. I got to the basement and quickly put my shirt one. I always came to work with the uniform on me. I got at the plaza at 4:07pm. The supervisor stopped me and told me where my post would be. He took two minutes of my time. I punched in at 4:10pm. I kept working for three hours straight and relief for break later on. I went to the basement; just eat my food and the supervisor called me. The supervisor wrote me up for being fifteen minutes late instead of ten minutes. The grace period was thirty minutes late. I read it and I did not sign anything. The supervisor accused me by saying that I used to come late when never did, but only this time. I always had to come to work early in case some of the guards did not want me to use their access card. The chief supervisor and other supervisors were the one who told me to use the other guards' access card and never told the guards that to make that happened without any issues. The supervisor called one of the guards on the radio to force him to say that I used to come late sometimes, even though the guard said not me. I did not blame the guard to be forced by the supervisor. I wanted to say something but decided not to because I already in trouble and I did not want to further that trouble. I decided to say that I never late. Therefore, the supervisor decided to send me home which I did not bother anyway. I took five classes that fall semester and was behind on my studies any way.

I went home just to catch up on my studies. I came to work on the next day which was on Sunday. The chief supervisor was there and he did not come to talk to me about what happened. I decided to bring the situation to him while I was on short break. I learned a big lesson from the chief supervisor. The chief supervisor told me that the supervisor tried to get me in trouble and I did not let it happened. I thought that the supervisor was acting stupidly due to power he had. I even told the chief supervisor to check the camera to see what time I came in, and did not want to do that. I told the chief supervisor that I just want to pay for the hours I just worked. I was surprised that I got paid the whole eight hours instead of three hours I worked. The chief supervisor even told me not to worry about anything. The chief supervisor did not appreciate that the supervisor sent me home. That was a problem because everyone seemed to get affected by small breaks and lunch relief on the absence of one person.

I explained the situation to the supervisor at school one day, the one who saved me to get my job back. He told me that they should have been happy for doing my job instead of firing me for doing it. The supervisor compared me with the security guard at school. The supervisor told me that someone went to report to the security office about that the guard let someone in without checking the person's ID, even though the guard saw when the person walked out and came back. Therefore, the guard lost his job over something that appeared not a problem.

The last event was one Sunday afternoon I had been told to do the point for four hours straight. I had been chosen because the regular guards who usually did the point did not show up to work that Sunday. I was the only among the other guards I worked with that day who could do the best out of it because the other guards came after me and still on training. I started to work and stopped someone. The person never told me that if he worked in the place, as well as being one of the bosses. He decided to call the chief supervisor on the radio. I decided to let him in. I saw him, the chief supervisor, and another chief of another group were talking about few kilometers from the booth where I stand. I saw them talking for few minute while kept looking at me and wondered what they talked about. I hope that everything was fine. I came to work next weekend which was on Saturday. I went to the basement and the supervisor who tried to get me in trouble said to me that not to bother because I was out of the schedule after what happened last Sunday. The decided to bring my countryman back to the place, the one who tried to get me in trouble, to replace me. I went to the point and the chief supervisor was there. The chief supervisor told me that it was not that I did not do my job. I did my job. The person that I stopped and did not know who he was decided to get me out of the place. The supervisor added that he did not appreciate what happened to me. He also added that the President might come here and tie his shoelace and laugh "AH AH" and everyone loses their job. I wondered was the chief supervisor sent me a message or not. One Sunday afternoon at the end of summer 2011, I met with my countryman, the one who was not a trouble maker, told me that he left two months after I let go. He told me that he knew what was going to happen and left before he got affected by it. He told me that everyone, including the supervisors, lost their jobs. The chief supervisor was the only one remained. The other company that took over absolutely decided to bring their own guards. Some of the guards who worked in the place for ten or over felt betrayed. I did not mind that the supervisors let go off because they come late and leave early, and every guard knew about that. It was absurd of one of them tried to write me up for lateness. There were cameras everywhere watching everything. These supervisors were careless about that. There was a small hidden camera discovered by the chief supervisor and he did not know who putted there. He was the only one knew where the camera was and the only one who could show others where it was. The chief supervisor stated that the camera is so small and look invisible to the eyes. The camera had been place where the security's office was and seemed to put it there to spy on security. Therefore, I was fire or lay off.

The third event took place in a condo that located in queens. I worked for the company just for nearly a year. It was on spring 2005 I got hired by the company when I started to go back to school. That was the beginning of my struggle to keep my head above water in school and in my private life. That event did not happen to me but being blame indirectly due to race issue. I used to work on the afternoon that summer and decided to work on the weekend due to school. There was this gentle man from East Europe and probably on his mid-fifties. He worked security on the morning shift. One day he told me that he used to be a physic professor back in his home country. He came to the U.S. and found out that he had to start from the scratch. He told me the time consuming, little language barrier, and his age which made him impossible to start all over. He also found that unfair to him. We talked and we show respect to each other. However, that changed one day when I came to work. I usually wave at him when I saw him patrol outside and he wave back. That day I wave and he did not wave. He gave me a look as if I was not existed, and look away. I spoke to the guard at the lobby about what happened to him. I did not get a clear and specific answer from the guard about what happened. I did not know who to blame of what happened unless I found what was going on which made the guard unhappy. I found if unfair for someone like that to condemn me in heart and mind of problem and issue that I absolutely did not have part of. We stay like that until the company went through changes and I got affected by those changes. Therefore, I was fired or lay off at the very end of year. There is something that I began to learn about race on the third event. The guard also dragged me down as well in a problem that I did not have part of due to my race. I wonder if he would accept the same predicament if someone else done the same to him. I began to find out that I held responsible and accountable for my brothers, sisters, and my countrymen's mess. Therefore, the same should apply for everyone else without favoritism and no exception if that is the case.

These three events reminded that I had to do a lot to deal with some human beings on their nastiness, brutality, ugliness, cleverness, ridiculousness, egomaniac, etc. I learned from my past to protect my present and future. The only way that one can deal with people like that is to have respect for himself or herself so that one should do the best to never get into any ridiculous situations with people like that. The worst thing is that they always intend to do so and blame those they affect with them. That is why there always going to be problem in marriages, friendships, and families, work, legal system, etc because people like that always intend to stir some trouble particularly when it is unnecessary and unwanted for them to do so. It seems to be that they do not feel good or great if they do not create, produce, or invent any kind of problems to affect others with. Therefore, how the legal system would be able to deal with people like that when some of them are really good to get away with wrongdoings. It is the responsibility of those who suffer from people like that to find ways to deal with people like that. There are two types of people I begin to pay attention on. The first types of people are the one who are wolves in sheep skins. The second types of people are the one who like to play angels and demons. Therefore, those who suffer have a lot of work to do to protect themselves in this world.

Printed in the United States
By Bookmasters